hooked on *fish*

100 recipes for all your fresh & canned fish favourites

THE AUSTRALIAN
Women's Weekly

contents

Seafood in general, be it fresh, smoked or canned, should be part of everybody's diet. Introduce fish to toddlers as early as possible, encourage children to eat fish and other seafood so it becomes a normal part of their diet. Most fresh seafood has a season when it's plentiful and at its best, and is cheap to buy – just like fruit and vegies. If your family eats seafood at least twice a week, the general health of everyone will benefit enormously.

Pamela Clark

Food Director

Fish contains omega-3 – the oilier the fish the more omega-3 it has. Omega-3 is a fatty acid that helps with brain function and protects the heart from disease. It must be obtained from food as the body cannot manufacture omega-3. That's why it's recommended you eat oily fish at least twice a week.

The no-fuss way to cook fish

Many people don't like to cook fish – they like to eat it in restaurants, but hate the smell of fish being cooked at home. The way around this is to cook fish in the oven in foil – to steam it – the nutrients are kept in the foil parcel, and the fishy smells can't escape – it's the best of both worlds. Use a cut lemon on your fingers, knives and cutting board and rinse thoroughly to get rid of fishy odours.

One (good) cook's manual

For those of you who don't mind the smell of fish, and/or have a great extractor fan in your kitchen, the world of fish is your oyster, so to speak. You can shallow-fry it, stir-fry it, deep-fry it, poach it, grill it, bake it and barbecue it. You can serve it raw, curried, stewed, in soups, salads, fishcakes, dips and sandwiches.

Buying seafood

When buying whole fish, look for shiny eyes. Dull eyes mean the fish has been sitting there for a while. Fillets and steaks should look moist, never dry. Fish should have a fresh "sea" smell. If it smells strongly of fish, don't buy it. Mussels are bought alive and their shells should be closed; don't buy any that are open – they are dead. Raw prawns should be shiny and not strong-smelling; scallops should be moist.

Storing seafood

Try to eat seafood on the day you buy it – if that's not possible, freeze it, wrapped very well or, if you're cooking it the next day and you're confident it will last, put the fish on a plate, cover it with foil or plastic wrap, and it store in the fridge.

poached fish cutlets with herb salad

We used blue-eye trevalla cutlets in this recipe, but you can use any white fish cutlets.

4 x 200g white fish cutlets
10cm stick fresh lemon grass (20g),
  halved lengthways
1 lime, sliced thickly

herb salad
50g baby asian greens
½ cup loosely packed fresh coriander leaves
⅓ cup loosely packed vietnamese mint leaves
⅓ cup loosely packed fresh mint leaves
⅓ cup loosely packed fresh dill sprigs

asian dressing
¼ cup (60ml) lime juice
2 tablespoons fish sauce
2 teaspoons peanut oil
2 teaspoons grated palm sugar
1 fresh small red thai chilli, chopped finely
1 clove garlic, chopped finely

1 Place fish, lemon grass and lime in large frying pan; barely cover fish with cold water. Bring slowly to a gentle simmer. Remove from heat; stand pan, covered, 10 minutes. Remove fish from liquid; drain.
2 Meanwhile, make herb salad and asian dressing.
3 Toss herb salad with half the dressing. Serve fish topped with salad; drizzle with remaining dressing.
herb salad Combine ingredients in medium bowl.
asian dressing Combine ingredients in screw-top jar; shake well.

prep + cook time **35 minutes** serves **4**
nutritional count per serving **6g total fat (1.6g saturated fat); 878kJ (210 cal); 3.2g carbohydrate; 34.4g protein; 1.8g fibre**

Vietnamese mint is not a mint, but a pungent and peppery narrow-leafed member of the buckwheat family. Also known as laksa leaf and cambodian mint, it is available from Asian greengrocers.

This dish is great with a watercress salad.

30g butter, softened

2 teaspoons finely chopped fresh
flat-leaf parsley

2 teaspoons rinsed, drained baby capers,
chopped finely

½ teaspoon finely grated lemon rind

1 drained anchovy fillet, chopped finely

4 x 180g salmon fillets, skin on

salmon and lemon and caper butter

1 Combine butter, parsley, capers, rind and anchovy in small bowl. Place mixture on plastic wrap, shape into a log; wrap tightly then freeze until firm.

2 Cook fish, skin-side down, in heated oiled large frying pan about 5 minutes or until skin is crisp. Turn fish, cook about 3 minutes. Remove fish from pan, cover; stand 5 minutes.

3 Serve fish with slices of lemon caper butter.

prep + cook time **20 minutes (+ freezing)**
serves **4**

nutritional count per serving **19g total fat** (6.9g saturated fat); 1308kJ (313 cal); 0.2g carbohydrate; 35.4g protein; 0.1g fibre

Serve with a green salad and lemon wedges, if you wish.
Soak bamboo skewers in water for at least an hour to prevent scorching during cooking. Yogurt, cream or milk can be used instead of the buttermilk.

4 x 180g salmon fillets, skin on
lemon grass mayo
10cm stick fresh lemon grass (20g), chopped coarsely
3 fresh kaffir lime leaves, chopped coarsely
1 teaspoon finely grated lemon rind
¼ cup (60ml) lemon juice
2 tablespoons mayonnaise
1 tablespoon buttermilk
1 fresh kaffir lime leaf, sliced finely
2 teaspoons warm water

salmon skewers with lemon grass mayo

1 Make lemon grass mayo.
2 Meanwhile, halve fish fillets lengthways, thread onto eight bamboo skewers.
3 Cook fish, skin-side down, in heated oiled large frying pan until skin is crisp. Turn skewers, cook about 2 minutes.
4 Serve skewers topped with lemon grass mayo.
lemon grass mayo Combine lemon grass, coarsely chopped lime leaves, rind and juice in small saucepan. Bring to the boil; reduce heat, simmer, uncovered, until mixture is reduced to about 1 tablespoon. Strain mixture into small bowl, discard solids. Cool mixture 10 minutes, then stir in mayonnaise, buttermilk, finely sliced lime leaf and the water.
prep + cook time **15 minutes** serves **4**
nutritional count per serving **16.1g total fat (3.3g saturated fat); 1246kJ (298 cal); 2.7g carbohydrate; 35.5g protein; 0.1g fibre**

400g fresh udon noodles
4 x 200g snapper fillets, skin on
1 tablespoon olive oil
2 cloves garlic, crushed
2 fresh long red chillies, sliced thinly
1cm piece fresh ginger (5g), grated
2 teaspoons finely grated lemon rind
2 tablespoons lemon juice
1 tablespoon fish sauce
4 green onions, sliced thinly
½ cup loosely packed fresh coriander leaves

snapper with chilli noodles

1 Place noodles in medium heatproof bowl, cover with boiling water; stand until tender, drain.
2 Meanwhile, cook fish, skin-side down, in heated oiled large frying pan about 5 minutes or until skin is crisp; turn fish, cook 3 minutes. Remove fish from pan; cover, stand 5 minutes.
3 Heat oil in same cleaned pan; cook garlic, chilli and ginger, stirring, until fragrant. Add noodles, rind, juice, sauce and half the onion; stir gently until noodles are heated through.
4 Serve fish with noodles; sprinkle with coriander and remaining onion.

prep + cook time **25 minutes** serves **4**
nutritional count per serving **26.5g total fat (10.7g saturated fat); 2874kJ (681 cal); 55g carbohydrate; 50.9g protein; 8.6g fibre**

¼ cup (60ml) chinese cooking wine
¼ cup (60ml) light soy sauce
2 teaspoons sesame oil
2 cloves garlic, crushed
4cm piece fresh ginger (20g), grated
1 teaspoon caster sugar
4 x 200g snapper fillets, skin on

coriander noodles
180g dried somen noodles
1½ cups firmly packed fresh coriander leaves
2cm piece fresh ginger (10g), sliced
1½ tablespoons peanut oil
1 tablespoon lime juice
½ teaspoon dried chilli flakes

ginger and soy fish with coriander noodles

1 Combine cooking wine, sauce, oil, garlic, ginger, sugar and fish in medium bowl.
2 Make coriander noodles.
3 Cook fish in heated oiled large frying pan until cooked through.
4 Serve fish with coriander noodles.
coriander noodles Cook noodles in large saucepan of boiling water until tender; drain reserving ¼ cup cooking liquid. Meanwhile, blend or process coriander, ginger, oil, juice and chilli until mixture forms a paste. Combine coriander paste, noodles and reserved cooking liquid in large bowl.
prep + cook time **25 minutes** serves **4**
nutritional count per serving **14.1g total fat (3.1g saturated fat); 1948kJ (466 cal); 33.4g carbohydrate; 47.4g protein; 2.4g fibre**

Chinese cooking wine (chinese rice wine or hao hsing) is made from fermented rice, wheat, salt and sugar. It is available from supermarkets and Asian food shops; use sherry if you can't find it.

snapper with onion and prosciutto

This dish is great with creamy mashed potato.

400g spring onions, trimmed,
   halved lengthways
1 medium lemon (140g), quartered
2 stalks fresh rosemary
4 x 200g snapper fillets, skin on, halved
4 slices prosciutto (60g), halved

rosemary marinade
2 tablespoons lemon juice
1 tablespoon olive oil
2 teaspoons finely chopped fresh rosemary
1 teaspoon fresh thyme leaves
1 clove garlic, crushed

1 Preheat oven to 220°C/200°C fan-forced. Heat oiled large shallow baking dish in oven.
2 Make rosemary marinade.
3 Combine onion, lemon, rosemary and rosemary marinade in large bowl; add fish, turn to coat in marinade. Place fish, skin-side down, in hot dish; top with onion mixture and prosciutto. Roast uncovered, about 20 minutes.
4 Divide onion mixture among serving plates; top with fish and coarsely chopped prosciutto.
rosemary marinade Combine ingredients in screw-top jar; shake well.

prep + cook time **35 minutes** serves **4**
nutritional count per serving **8.9g total fat**
(2.2g saturated fat); 1179kJ (282 cal);
4.2g carbohydrate; 44.8g protein; 2.3g fibre

fish curry

We used blue-eye trevalla fillets in this recipe.

2 tablespoons olive oil
1 large brown onion (200g), sliced thinly
5cm piece fresh ginger (25g), grated
3 cloves garlic, crushed
1 teaspoon brown sugar
2 teaspoons garam marsala
2 teaspoons sweet paprika
1½ teaspoons ground turmeric
½ cup (125ml) chicken stock
1 cup (250ml) buttermilk
4 x 200g white fish fillets
steamed jasmine rice
1 cup (200g) jasmine rice
2 cups (500ml) water

1 Heat half the oil in medium saucepan; cook onion, ginger, garlic and sugar, stirring, until caramelised lightly. Add spices; cook, stirring, until fragrant.
2 Add stock to pan; bring to the boil. Reduce heat; simmer, uncovered, about 2 minutes or until slightly thickened. Add buttermilk; cook, stirring, 1 minute.
3 Make steamed jasmine rice.
4 Heat remaining oil in large frying pan; cook fish until browned both sides and cooked through.
5 Divide rice among serving bowls; top with fish and curry sauce. Sprinkle with fresh coriander leaves, if you like.
steamed jasmine rice Rinse rice under cold water until water runs clear; drain. Bring the water to the boil, covered, in medium saucepan; add rice. Cook, covered, over low heat, 10 minutes. Remove from heat; stand, covered, 10 minutes. Fluff rice with fork.
prep + cook time **35 minutes** serves **4**
nutritional count per serving **15.3g total fat (3.7g saturated fat); 2195kJ (525 cal); 47.2g carbohydrate; 48.1g protein; 1.6g fibre**

We used flathead fillets for this recipe. Serve with a green salad and lemon wedges, if you like.

1.5kg potatoes
vegetable oil, for deep-frying
8 white fish fillets (960g)

batter
¼ cup (35g) plain flour
¼ cup (35g) self-raising flour
⅓ cup (80ml) warm water
1 egg, separated
1 tablespoon vegetable oil

tartare sauce
2 tablespoons mayonnaise
1 tablespoon buttermilk
1 shallot (25g), chopped finely
1 tablespoon finely chopped cornichons
2 teaspoons rinsed, drained capers, chopped finely
2 teaspoons finely chopped fresh flat-leaf parsley
2 teaspoons lemon juice

fish and chips

1 Make batter.
2 Cut potatoes lengthways into 1cm chips; stand in large bowl of cold water 30 minutes.
3 Meanwhile, make tartare sauce.
4 Drain chips; pat dry. Heat oil in large deep saucepan; cook chips, in three batches, about 4 minutes or until soft but not browned. Drain.
5 Reheat oil; cook chips, in three batches, until crisp and golden brown, drain. Dip fish in batter; cook, in batches, until brown. Drain.
6 Serve fish with chips and tartare sauce.
batter Sift flours into medium bowl. Gradually whisk in water, egg yolk and oil until smooth. Cover; stand 30 minutes. Beat egg white in small bowl with electric mixer until soft peaks form. Fold egg white into batter, in two batches.
tartare sauce Combine ingredients in small bowl.
prep + cook time **1 hour 10 minutes (+ standing)** serves **4**
nutritional count per serving **40g total fat (6.3g saturated fat); 3465kJ (829 cal); 54.3g carbohydrate; 60.1g protein; 5.8g fibre**

We used whiting fillets in this recipe.

1kg mussels
2½ cups (625ml) water
1½ cups (375ml) fish stock
2 tablespoons olive oil
1 large brown onion (200g), chopped finely
2 cloves garlic, crushed
1½ cups (300g) arborio rice

½ cup (125ml) dry white wine
2 tablespoons tomato paste
2 bay leaves
500g uncooked medium king prawns, shelled, deveined, chopped coarsely
2 tablespoons coarsely chopped fresh flat-leaf parsley
4 x 120g white fish fillets, skin on, halved crossways

oven-baked seafood risotto

1 Preheat oven to 200°C/180°C fan-forced.
2 Scrub mussels; remove beards. Bring the water and stock to the boil in large saucepan. Add mussels; simmer, covered, about 3 minutes or until mussels open (discard any that do not). Remove mussels from liquid; reserve liquid. Remove the flesh from shells; discard shells.
3 Heat half the oil in large flameproof dish; cook onion and garlic, stirring, until onion is softened. Stir in rice then wine and paste; stir 1 minute. Add reserved stock mixture and bay leaves; bring to the boil. Cover dish tightly with lid or foil; place in oven. Cook 20 minutes.
4 Remove from oven; stir in prawns, mussels and half the parsley. Cover; stand 10 minutes.
5 Heat remaining oil in large frying pan; cook fish until cooked through. Serve risotto topped with fish and remaining parsley.

prep + cook time **50 minutes** serves **4**
nutritional count per serving **13.7g total fat (2.7g saturated fat); 2592kJ (620 cal); 66.3g carbohydrate; 50.5g protein; 2.1g fibre**

Coulibiac is basically a layered fish pie. You can prepare and refrigerate the individual layers the day before cooking, then simply assemble and bake when required. If the ocean trout fillet is too long, tuck the tail under to make the fillet a similar thickness all the way through.
This recipe is delicious with a rocket salad.

1 tablespoon olive oil
1 small brown onion (80g), chopped finely
1 clove garlic, crushed
1 cup (200g) jasmine rice
1 cup (250ml) fish stock
1 cup (250ml) water
1 bunch spinach (500g), trimmed
200g swiss brown mushrooms, sliced thinly
2 shallots (50g), sliced thinly
9 sheets fillo pastry
cooking-oil spray
1 egg white
650g ocean trout fillet, skin removed

coulibiac

1 Heat half the oil in medium saucepan; cook onion and garlic until soft. Stir in rice, then add stock and the water; bring to the boil. Simmer, covered, 15 minutes. Stand, covered, 5 minutes.
2 Boil, steam or microwave spinach until wilted. Rinse, drain; squeeze out liquid. Chop coarsely.
3 Heat remaining oil in large frying pan; cook mushrooms and shallot until browned lightly.
4 Preheat oven to 220°C/200°C fan-forced.
5 Spray pastry sheets with oil; fold into a 25cm square. Stack 3 squares, spraying each layer with oil. Place one stack on baking-paper-lined oven tray, brush with egg white; layer rice, mushroom, spinach then trout, leaving 2cm border. Overlap remaining squares over trout; fold pastry to seal. Cut slits in top; brush with egg white. Bake about 30 minutes; stand 20 minutes before serving.
prep + cook time **1 hour 20 minutes**
(+ standing) serves **6**
nutritional count per serving **8.4g total fat (1.3g saturated fat); 1492kJ (357 cal); 39.4g carbohydrate; 28.7g protein; 3.1g fibre**

Serve the soup with warm crusty bread to mop up the juices.

1 tablespoon olive oil
1 small fennel bulb (200g), sliced thinly
1 medium brown onion (150g), sliced thinly
3 cloves garlic, crushed
pinch saffron threads
1 tablespoon tomato paste
½ cup (125ml) dry white wine
810g can crushed tomatoes
2 cups (500ml) fish stock
2½ cups (625ml) water
1 teaspoon fresh thyme leaves
6 fresh sage leaves
1kg mussels
600g snapper fillets, cut into 3cm pieces
500g squid hoods, sliced thickly
¼ cup loosely packed fresh baby basil leaves

fish soup

1 Heat oil in large saucepan. Add fennel, onion and garlic; cook, stirring, until vegetables soften. Add saffron, paste and wine; cook, stirring, 2 minutes.
2 Add tomatoes, stock, the water, thyme and sage to pan; bring to the boil. Reduce heat; simmer, covered, 20 minutes.
3 Meanwhile, scrub mussels; remove beards.
4 Blend or process soup, in batches, until smooth. Return soup to same pan; bring to the boil. Add mussels, fish and squid; cook, covered, about 3 minutes or until mussels open (discard any that do not).
5 Divide soup among serving bowls; sprinkle with basil.

prep + cook time **50 minutes** serves 6
nutritional count per serving 7.4g total fat **(1.7g saturated fat); 1200kJ (287 cal); 8.9g carbohydrate; 41.1g protein; 2.9g fibre**

chermoula-crusted fish

We used barramundi fillets in this recipe.

½ cup (35g) stale breadcrumbs
2 tablespoons finely chopped fresh
    flat-leaf parsley
2 tablespoons finely chopped fresh coriander
2 cloves garlic, crushed
1cm piece fresh ginger (5g), grated finely
½ teaspoon finely grated lemon rind
1 teaspoon ground cumin
1 teaspoon sweet paprika
1 tablespoon olive oil
4 x 200g white fish fillets
80g mesclun
1 medium lemon (140g), cut into wedges

1 Preheat oven to 220°C/200°C fan-forced.
Oil oven tray; line with baking paper.
2 Combine breadcrumbs, herbs, garlic, ginger,
rind, spices and oil in medium bowl. Place fish
on tray; press breadcrumb mixture onto fish.
3 Roast fish, uncovered, about 15 minutes, or
until cooked through.
4 Serve fish with mesclun and lemon wedges.
prep + cook time 30 minutes serves 4
nutritional count per serving 9.4g total fat
(2.1g saturated fat); 1200kJ (287 cal);
6.8g carbohydrate; 42.6g protein; 1.8g fibre

crunchy wasabi-crusted fish fillets

We used blue-eye trevalla fillets in this recipe.

4 x 200g white fish fillets
2 tablespoons mayonnaise
2 teaspoons wasabi
½ cup (35g) japanese breadcrumbs
cooking-oil spray
red cabbage coleslaw
2 tablespoons rice vinegar
2 teaspoons vegetable oil
1 teaspoon caster sugar
½ teaspoon mustard powder
¼ small red cabbage (300g), shredded finely
1 lebanese cucumber (130g), seeded,
  sliced thinly
4 green onions, sliced thinly

1 Preheat oven to 220°C/200°C fan-forced. Oil oven tray; line with baking paper.
2 Place fish on tray; spread with combined mayonnaise and wasabi. Press breadcrumbs onto fish. Spray lightly with oil. Roast, uncovered, about 15 minutes or until cooked through.
3 Meanwhile, make red cabbage coleslaw. Serve with fish.
red cabbage coleslaw Whisk vinegar, oil, sugar and mustard in medium bowl. Add cabbage, cucumber and onion; mix well.

prep + cook time **30 minutes** serves **4**
nutritional count per serving 12.5g **total fat** (2.4g saturated fat); 1442kJ (345 cal); 12.7g carbohydrate; 44.3g protein; 3.7g fibre

This dish would be good served with roasted baby potatoes and steamed broccolini.

4 x 200g snapper fillets
½ cup (125ml) dry white wine
20g butter, chopped
½ cup coarsely chopped fresh flat-leaf parsley
2 tablespoons rinsed, drained baby capers

pan-seared snapper with buttery capers

1 Cook fish, skin-side down, in heated oiled large frying pan about 5 minutes; turn fish, cook about 3 minutes. Remove from pan; cover, stand 5 minutes.
2 Add wine to pan, bring to the boil; boil until liquid is reduced by half. Stir in butter, parsley and capers.
3 Serve fish drizzled with buttery capers.
prep + cook time 25 minutes serves 4
nutritional count per serving 7.3g total fat (3.9g saturated fat); 1066kJ (255 cal); 0.8g carbohydrate; 40.9g protein; 0.5g fibre

Soak skewers in cold water for at least an hour before using to prevent them from scorching during cooking.

1 litre (4 cups) water
1 cup (170g) polenta
20g butter
800g snapper fillets, cut into 3cm pieces
80g baby spinach leaves

tarragon vinaigrette
¼ cup (60ml) white wine vinegar
2 tablespoons olive oil
1 shallot (25g), chopped finely
1 tablespoon dijon mustard
1 tablespoon finely chopped fresh tarragon
½ teaspoon caster sugar

snapper skewers with tarragon vinaigrette

1 Oil deep 19cm-square cake pan; line base and sides with baking paper.
2 Place the water in medium saucepan; bring to the boil. Gradually stir in polenta. Reduce heat; cook, stirring, about 10 minutes or until polenta thickens. Stir in butter; spread into pan. Cover; refrigerate 3 hours or overnight.
3 Turn polenta onto board, trim edges; cut into four squares then into triangles. Cook on heated oiled grill plate until heated through.
4 Meanwhile, thread fish onto eight bamboo skewers. Cook on heated oiled grill plate until browned and cooked as you like.
5 Make tarragon vinaigrette.
6 Serve kebabs with polenta and spinach; drizzle with vinaigrette.
tarragon vinaigrette Combine ingredients in screw-top jar; shake well.
prep + cook time **40 minutes** (+ **refrigeration**) serves **4**
nutritional count per serving **17.4g total fat (5.3g saturated fat); 1935kJ (463 cal); 30.3g carbohydrate; 44.8g protein; 2g fibre**

1kg kipfler potatoes, chopped coarsely
20g butter
2 teaspoons olive oil
4 x 175g tuna steaks
80g baby rocket leaves
basil pesto
1 cup firmly packed fresh basil leaves
1 tablespoon finely grated parmesan cheese
1 clove garlic, quartered
2 tablespoons lemon juice
1 tablespoon olive oil

tuna with basil pesto

1 Preheat oven to 220°C/200°C fan-forced. Oil oven tray; line with baking paper.
2 Boil, steam or microwave potato until tender; drain. Mash potato coarsely in large bowl with butter. Place potato on tray; drizzle with oil. Roast, uncovered, in oven, about 30 minutes.
3 Meanwhile, make basil pesto.
4 Cook fish on heated oiled grill plate (or grill or barbecue) until cooked as desired.
5 Divide rocket and potato among serving plates; top with fish and pesto.
basil pesto Blend or process ingredients until just combined.
prep + cook time **45 minutes** serves **4**
nutritional count per serving **21.9g total fat (8g saturated fat); 2299kJ (550 cal); 33.7g carbohydrate; 51.4g protein; 5.7g fibre**

800g baby new potatoes, halved
4 x 180g ocean trout fillets, skin on
1 teaspoon peppercorn medley, crushed
½ teaspoon sea salt flakes
2 tablespoons lemon juice
2 tablespoons horseradish cream
¼ cup coarsely chopped fresh dill
150g watercress, trimmed

salt and pepper trout

1 Boil, steam or microwave potato until tender; drain. Cover to keep warm.
2 Score skin on fillets three times; coat skin with combined pepper and salt. Cook fish, skin-side down, in heated oiled large frying pan, about 5 minutes or until browned and crisp. Turn fish; cook about 3 minutes or until cooked through.
3 Meanwhile, combine juice, horseradish and dill with potato in large bowl.
4 Serve fish with potato mixture and watercress.
prep + cook time **30 minutes** serves **4**
nutritional count per serving **4.1g total fat
(1.6g saturated fat); 1359kJ (325 cal);
28.3g carbohydrate; 40.3g protein; 5.2g fibre**

niçoise tasting plate

We used dutch cream potatoes and yellow-fin tuna in this recipe.

4 small potatoes (480g)
200g baby green beans, trimmed
2 x 250g tuna steaks, halved crossways
1 baby cos lettuce (180g), quartered lengthways
200g grape tomatoes, halved
2 tablespoons rinsed, drained baby capers
½ cup (90g) baby black olives, seeded
8 drained anchovy fillets
2 hard-boiled eggs, sliced thinly
garlic mustard dressing
¼ cup (60ml) red wine vinegar
2 tablespoons olive oil
1 small clove garlic, crushed
1 teaspoon dijon mustard

1 Boil, steam or microwave potatoes until tender; drain. Slice thinly.
2 Boil, steam or microwave beans until tender; drain. Rinse under cold water; drain.
3 Make garlic mustard dressing.
4 Cook tuna on heated oiled grill plate (or grill or barbecue) until cooked as desired.
5 Divide lettuce among serving plates; arrange potato, beans, tomato, capers, olives, anchovies and eggs in separate stacks. Top with tuna; drizzle with dressing.
garlic mustard dressing Combine ingredients in screw-top jar; shake well.
prep + cook time **35 minutes** serves **4**
nutritional count per serving **20.2g total fat (5.2g saturated fat); 1923kJ (460 cal); 24.7g carbohydrate; 42g protein; 6g fibre**

fish with polenta and dill gremolata

We used barramundi fillets in this recipe.

2 cups (500ml) chicken stock
1 cup (250ml) milk
½ cup (85g) instant polenta
¼ cup (20g) finely grated parmesan cheese
4 x 200g white fish fillets, skin on
dill gremolata
1 teaspoon finely grated orange rind
2 cloves garlic, chopped finely
½ cup coarsely chopped fresh dill
¼ cup coarsely chopped fresh flat-leaf parsley

1 Make dill gremolata.
2 Combine stock and milk in large saucepan, bring to the boil; gradually stir in polenta. Reduce heat; cook, stirring, about 10 minutes or until polenta thickens. Remove from heat; stir in cheese.
3 Meanwhile, cook fish in heated oiled large frying pan. Serve with polenta; sprinkle over gremolata.
dill gremolata Combine ingredients in small bowl.
prep + cook time **30 minutes** serves **4**
nutritional count per serving **9.5g total fat** (4.4g saturated fat); 1501kJ (359 cal); 18.9g carbohydrate; 48.4g protein; 1.6g fibre

375g salmon fillet
⅓ cup (75g) firmly packed brown sugar
¼ cup (70g) coarse cooking salt
2 tablespoons sweet sherry
½ teaspoon five-spice powder
1 tablespoon lime juice
100g baby asian greens
2 lebanese cucumbers (260g),
   seeded, sliced thinly

asian dressing
1 tablespoon light soy sauce
2 teaspoons water
2 teaspoons sweet sherry
2 teaspoons lime juice
1 clove garlic, crushed
1 fresh small red thai chilli, chopped finely
½ teaspoon caster sugar

asian-style cured salmon salad

1 Remove skin, bones and any fat from fish.
2 Combine sugar, salt, sherry, five-spice and juice in medium bowl. Add fish; turn to coat in mixture. Cover; refrigerate overnight.
3 Make asian dressing.
4 Wash fish; pat dry. Slice fish thinly.
5 Combine asian greens, cucumber and dressing in large bowl. Divide salad among serving plates; top with cured salmon.
asian dressing Combine ingredients in screw-top jar; shake well.
prep time **20 minutes (+ refrigeration)** serves **4**
nutritional count per serving **6.8g total fat (1.5g saturated fat); 970kJ (232 cal); 20.6g carbohydrate; 18.9g protein; 1.1g fibre**

We used flathead fillets in this recipe.

fish burritos

1 cup coarsely chopped fresh coriander
2 teaspoons finely chopped coriander root
  and stem mixture
1 fresh long red chilli, chopped coarsely
1 clove garlic, quartered
1½ teaspoons sweet paprika
1 teaspoon ground cumin
⅓ cup (80ml) olive oil
800g small white fish fillets, halved
8 x 20cm round flour tortillas
1 baby cos lettuce (180g), leaves separated
1 lebanese cucumber (130g), sliced thinly
lime buttermilk dressing
¼ cup (60ml) buttermilk
1 teaspoon finely grated lime rind
2 teaspoons lime juice

1 Blend or process coriander leaves, root and stem mixture, chilli, garlic, paprika, cumin and ¼ cup of the oil until smooth. Combine coriander mixture and fish in large bowl. Cover; refrigerate 30 minutes.
2 Meanwhile, make lime buttermilk dressing.
3 Heat remaining oil in large frying pan; cook fish, in batches, until browned both sides and cooked through. Cover to keep warm.
4 Meanwhile, warm tortillas following directions on packet.
5 Divide fish, dressing, lettuce and cucumber among tortillas; wrap to enclose filling.
lime buttermilk dressing Combine ingredients in small jug.
prep + cook time **30 minutes**
(+ refrigeration) makes **8**
nutritional count per burrito **14g total fat (2.5g saturated fat); 1267kJ (303 cal); 19g carbohydrate; 24.3g protein; 2g fibre**

400g can chickpeas, rinsed, drained
2 tablespoons lemon juice
2 tablespoons warm water
1 tablespoon olive oil
1 clove garlic, chopped
pinch cayenne pepper
4 x 200g salmon cutlets

rocket salad
50g baby rocket leaves
1 tablespoon red wine vinegar
1 tablespoon olive oil
½ cup (90g) baby black olives, seeded
2 shallots (50g), sliced thinly

salmon cutlets with lemon chickpea purée

1 Make rocket salad.
2 Blend or process chickpeas, juice, the water, oil, garlic and cayenne pepper until smooth.
3 Cook fish in heated oiled large frying pan.
4 Meanwhile, heat chickpea purée in medium saucepan until mixture is just warmed though.
5 Serve fish with warmed chickpea purée and rocket salad.

rocket salad Toss ingredients in medium bowl.

prep + cook time **35 minutes** serves **4**
nutritional count per serving 22.2g total fat (4.1g saturated fat); 1718kJ (411 cal); 15g carbohydrate; 36.1g protein; 3.8g fibre

We used blue-eye trevalla in this recipe.

2 tablespoons olive oil
600g kipfler potatoes, sliced thickly
2 medium leeks (700g), sliced thickly
4 cloves garlic, bruised
pinch saffron threads
2 cups (500ml) chicken stock
4 x 200g white fish fillets

baked fish with saffron, leek and potato

1 Preheat oven to 220°C/200°C fan-forced.
2 Heat oil in large flameproof dish; cook potato, leek and garlic, stirring, until leek is soft. Add saffron and stock; bring to the boil. Reduce heat; simmer, uncovered, 10 minutes. Add fish, cover, transfer to oven.
3 Bake fish 20 minutes or until cooked through.
4 Serve fish topped with potato and leek; drizzle with pan juices. Sprinkle fish with fresh chervil leaves, if you like.

prep + cook time 35 minutes serves 4
nutritional count per serving 14.6g total fat (3g saturated fat); 1831kJ (438 cal); 24.9g carbohydrate; 48.1g protein; 6.6g fibre

char-grilled tuna with tomato salad

2 tablespoons lemon juice
2 tablespoons olive oil
2 teaspoons dijon mustard
4 medium tomatoes (600g), seeded,
  chopped coarsely
½ medium red onion (85g), sliced thinly
4 x 200g tuna steaks
60g baby rocket leaves

1 Combine juice, oil and mustard in medium bowl; stir in tomato and onion.
2 Cook tuna on heated oiled grill plate (or grill or barbecue) until cooked as desired.
3 Gently toss rocket through tomato mixture; serve with tuna.

prep + cook time 20 minutes serves 4
nutritional count per serving 20.8g total fat (5.9g saturated fat); 1760kJ (421 cal); 4.7g carbohydrate; 52.5g protein; 2.4g fibre

salmon spinach fillo parcels

500g spinach, trimmed
cooking-oil spray
4 sheets fillo pastry
4 x 160g salmon fillets
2 cups (520g) bottled tomato pasta sauce

1 Preheat oven to 220°C/200°C fan-forced.
Oil oven tray; line with baking paper.
2 Boil, steam or microwave spinach until wilted.
Rinse under cold water; drain. Squeeze out excess
liquid; chop coarsely.

3 Spray each sheet of pastry with oil. Fold each
sheet in half widthways. Place one sheet on board;
centre one salmon fillet on pastry, top with a
quarter of the spinach. Fold in sides of pastry and
roll to enclose filling. Spray parcel with oil; place
on tray, seam-side down. Repeat to make three
more parcels.
4 Bake parcels about 15 minutes or until pastry
is browned lightly and fish is cooked through.
5 Bring sauce to the boil in small saucepan. Serve
with parcels.

prep + cook time 40 minutes serves 4
nutritional count per serving 14.8g total fat
(2.9g saturated fat); 1534kJ (367 cal);
20.2g carbohydrate; 36g protein; 4.4g fibre

2 x 200g salmon fillets, skin on
2 cups (500ml) fish stock
2 tablespoons light soy sauce
2 tablespoons brown rice vinegar
1 tablespoon peanut oil
2 teaspoons caster sugar
2 cups firmly packed watercress, trimmed
2 cups (160g) bean sprouts
2 cups (160g) finely shredded wombok
4 green onions, sliced thinly
2 fresh long red chillies, chopped finely

salmon with watercress salad

1 Combine fish and stock in medium saucepan; bring to the boil. Reduce heat, simmer 1 minute. Remove from heat. Stand, covered, 10 minutes.
2 Meanwhile, combine sauce, vinegar, oil and sugar in large bowl. Add watercress, sprouts, wombok, onion and chilli; mix gently.
3 Drain fish, remove skin; flake fish over salad.
prep + cook time 25 minutes serves 4
nutritional count per serving 19.2g total fat (4.2g saturated fat); 1542kJ (369 cal); 4.9g carbohydrate; 43.1g protein; 2.3g fibre

Brown rice vinegar, made from brown rice, has been called the eastern version of apple cider vinegar, although its mild flavour has a subtle sweetness and about half the sharpness. It is available from Asian grocery stores and some health-food stores.

Use coral or ocean trout in this recipe, or your favourite white fish.

1 tablespoon coriander seeds
⅔ cup (50g) stale sourdough breadcrumbs
2 teaspoons finely chopped coriander root and
    stem mixture
1 tablespoon finely chopped fresh
    coriander leaves
1 tablespoon finely chopped fresh chives
2 teaspoons finely grated lemon rind
20g butter, melted
1 tablespoon olive oil
4 x 200g ocean trout fillets

asian salad
2 tablespoons lemon juice
1 tablespoon olive oil
2 teaspoons dijon mustard
½ teaspoon caster sugar
100g baby asian greens

roast trout with spicy herb crust

1 Dry-fry coriander seeds in heated small frying pan, stirring, until fragrant. Using mortar and pestle, crush seeds until ground finely.
2 Preheat oven to 220°C/200°C fan-forced. Oil oven tray; line with baking paper.
3 Combine crushed seeds with breadcrumbs, coriander root and stem mixture, chopped coriander, chives, rind, butter and oil in medium bowl. Place fish on tray; press breadcrumb mixture onto fish. Roast, uncovered, about 15 minutes or until fish is cooked through.
4 Meanwhile, make asian salad. Serve salad with fish.
asian salad Combine juice, oil, mustard and sugar in screw-top jar; shake well. Combine asian greens and dressing in large bowl.
prep + cook time 30 minutes serves 4
nutritional count per serving 16.7g total fat (5g saturated fat); 1425kJ (341 cal); 6.9g carbohydrate; 40.1g protein; 1.3g fibre

We used kingfish fillets in this recipe.

¼ cup (60ml) orange juice
1 tablespoon dijon mustard
2 teaspoons olive oil
4 x 200g white fish fillets, skin on
iceberg salad
2 lebanese cucumbers (260g), seeded,
   sliced thinly
3 cups (180g) finely shredded iceberg lettuce
1 tablespoon finely shredded fresh mint
1 medium orange (240g), segmented
½ cup coarsely chopped fresh flat-leaf parsley
1 tablespoon olive oil
1 tablespoon white wine vinegar

orange and mustard-glazed fish

1 Preheat oven to 240°C/220°C fan-forced.
Oil oven tray; line with baking paper.
2 Combine juice, mustard, oil and fish in
medium bowl.
3 Make iceberg salad.
4 Place fish on tray; roast about 12 minutes
or until fish is cooked through. Serve with
iceberg salad.
iceberg salad Combine ingredients in large bowl.
prep + cook time **35 minutes** serves **4**
nutritional count per serving **11.5g total fat
(2.3g saturated fat); 1262kJ (302 cal);
5.9g carbohydrate; 42.3g protein; 2.7g fibre**

⅓ cup (80ml) light soy sauce
2 tablespoons oyster sauce
⅓ cup (80ml) mirin
2 tablespoons sake
2 teaspoons caster sugar
4 x 180g salmon fillets, skin on

udon salad
180g dried udon noodles
2 teaspoons vegetable oil
2 teaspoons sesame oil
2 tablespoons thinly sliced garlic chives
2 lebanese cucumbers (260g), seeded, cut
  into matchsticks
3 green onions, thinly sliced
1 tablespoon toasted sesame seeds

teriyaki salmon with udon salad

1 Combine sauces, mirin, sake and sugar in large bowl, add fish; turn to coat in marinade. Stand 10 minutes then drain; reserve marinade.
2 Cook fish, skin-side down, in heated oiled large frying pan about 5 minutes or until crisp; turn fish, cook about 5 minutes. Remove fish from pan; cover, stand 5 minutes.
3 Meanwhile, bring reserved marinade to the boil in small saucepan; reduce heat, simmer, uncovered, about 5 minutes or until sauce is thickened slightly.
4 Meanwhile, make udon salad. Serve salad with fish; drizzle with sauce.
udon salad Cook noodles in large saucepan of boiling water until tender; drain. Rinse under cold water; drain. Return noodles to pan with remaining ingredients; toss to combine.
prep + cook time **25 minutes** serves **4**
nutritional count per serving **19.6g total fat (3.8g saturated fat); 2203kJ (527 cal); 38.2g carbohydrate; 42.7g protein; 2.5g fibre**

fish gyros

We used flathead fillets in this recipe.
Soak bamboo skewers in cold water for
at least an hour before using to prevent
them scorching during cooking.

2 tablespoons olive oil
1 tablespoon red wine vinegar
2 medium tomatoes (300g),
    cut into thin wedges
50g baby rocket leaves
4 x 110g long thin white fish fillets, halved
1 tablespoon finely chopped fresh oregano
4 x 20cm flour tortillas
½ cup (140g) yogurt
1 clove garlic, crushed

1 Combine half the oil with vinegar, tomato and rocket in medium bowl.

2 Combine fish, oregano and remaining oil in medium bowl. Thread fish lengthways onto eight bamboo skewers. Cook skewers on heated oiled grill plate (or grill or barbecue) until cooked.

3 Wrap tortillas in foil; warm on heated grill plate about 2 minutes, turning once, or until heated through.

4 Serve warm tortillas topped with fish and salad; drizzle with combined yogurt and garlic.

prep + cook time 30 minutes serves 4
nutritional count per serving 15.3g total fat
(3.2g saturated fat); 1417kJ (339 cal);
21g carbohydrate; 28.1g protein; 2.3g fibre

grilled fish kebabs

We used thick-cut ling fillets in this recipe. Soak skewers in cold water for at least an hour before using, to prevent scorching during cooking.

1kg white fish fillets
2 medium zucchini (240g)
1 medium red capsicum (200g)
1 medium red onion (170g)
1 cup (250g) yogurt
2 tablespoons lemon juice
3 cloves garlic, crushed
2 teaspoons ground cumin
2 teaspoons ground coriander
1 teaspoon sweet paprika
½ cup loosely packed fresh coriander leaves

1 Cut fish, zucchini and capsicum into similar-sized chunks; cut onion into wedges. Thread ingredients onto eight bamboo skewers.
2 Cook skewers on heated oiled grill plate (or grill or barbecue) about 10 minutes.
3 Meanwhile, combine yogurt, juice, garlic and spices in small bowl.
4 Serve skewers topped with yogurt mixture; sprinkle with fresh coriander.

prep + cook time **30 minutes** makes **8**
nutritional count per kebab **4g total fat**
(1.6g saturated fat); 706kJ (169 cal);
4.3g carbohydrate; 28.1g protein; 1.3g fibre

We used skinless ling fillets in this recipe.

1½ cups (330g) risoni pasta
1 cup (120g) frozen peas
150g sugar snap peas, trimmed
200g baby green beans, trimmed,
    halved crossways
1 cup (250ml) dry white wine
1½ cups (375ml) fish stock

600g white fish fillets, cut into 3cm pieces
600g small squid hoods, sliced into rings
2 tablespoons olive oil
2 cloves garlic, crushed
4 drained anchovy fillets, chopped finely
2 teaspoons finely grated lemon rind
2 tablespoons lemon juice
½ cup coarsely chopped fresh flat-leaf parsley

summer seafood salad

1 Cook pasta in large saucepan of boiling water until tender; drain. Rinse under cold water; drain well.
2 Meanwhile, cook peas and beans in large saucepan of boiling water until tender; drain. Rinse under cold water; drain.
3 Heat wine and stock in large saucepan; bring to the boil. Add fish; reduce heat, simmer 2 minutes. Add squid; cook 2 minutes or until tender, drain.
4 Combine oil, garlic, anchovy, rind and juice in large bowl. Gently stir in pasta, vegetables and warm seafood; sprinkle with parsley.
prep + cook time 35 minutes   serves 4
nutritional count per serving   1.4g total fat (0.3g saturated fat); 1568kJ (375 cal); 61.7g carbohydrate; 14.4g protein; 6.7g fibre

This dish goes well with steamed jasmine rice.

2 tablespoons kecap manis
2 cloves garlic, crushed
1 tablespoon lime juice
2 teaspoons sambal oelek
4 x 200g ocean trout cutlets
1 tablespoon peanut oil
350g green beans, trimmed
4 green onions, sliced thinly

ocean trout with stir-fried beans

1 Combine kecap manis, garlic, juice and sambal in medium bowl, add fish; turn fish to coat in marinade.

2 Heat half the oil in large frying pan; cook fish until cooked through. Remove fish from pan; cover to keep warm.

3 Heat remaining oil in same pan; stir-fry beans and onion until tender. Serve with fish.

prep + cook time **25 minutes** serves **4**
nutritional count per serving **7.8g total fat (1.8g saturated fat); 1070kJ (256 cal); 3.5g carbohydrate; 41.2g protein; 2.8g fibre**

350g piece sashimi tuna
350g piece sashimi salmon
350g piece sashimi white fish
⅔ cup (160ml) lemon juice
⅓ cup (80ml) lime juice
⅓ cup (80ml) olive oil
1 clove garlic, chopped finely
1 tablespoon coarsely chopped small fresh basil leaves
2 teaspoons finely chopped fresh chives
2 tablespoons finely chopped walnuts
2 teaspoons rinsed, drained baby capers, chopped finely
2 teaspoons finely chopped fresh dill
2 teaspoons rice vinegar
2 green onions, chopped finely
1 fresh long red chilli, chopped finely

carpaccio trio

It's important to buy sashimi-quality fish for this recipe. We used kingfish as well as the tuna and salmon in this recipe. Ask your fishmonger for the best sashimi-quality white fish available that day.

1 Tightly wrap each piece of fish, separately, in plastic wrap; freeze about 1 hour or until slightly firm.
2 Unwrap fish then slice as thinly as possible. Arrange slices on separate serving platters; drizzle tuna and salmon with lemon juice, drizzle white fish with lime juice. Cover platters; refrigerate 1 hour.
3 Divide oil among three small bowls. Add garlic, basil and chives to one bowl. Add walnuts, capers and dill to another bowl. Add vinegar, onion and chilli to remaining bowl.
4 Drain excess juice from platters. To serve, divide fish among serving plates; drizzle tuna with basil mixture; salmon with walnut mixture and white fish with chilli mixture.

prep time **50 minutes (+ freezing and refrigeration)** serves 6
nutritional count per serving **23.1g total fat (4.5g saturated fat); 1538kJ (368 cal); 1.3g carbohydrate; 38.8g protein; 0.5g fibre**

1 tablespoon olive oil
1 cup (70g) stale breadcrumbs
½ teaspoon dried chilli flakes
1 teaspoon finely grated lime rind
4 x 200g ocean trout fillets

crunchy nut slaw
2 tablespoons lime juice
1 tablespoon vegetable oil
1 tablespoon fish sauce
½ cup (75g) coarsely chopped
  roasted unsalted cashews
½ cup coarsely chopped fresh coriander
2 cups (160g) shredded wombok

crumbed ocean trout
with crunchy nut slaw

1 Preheat oven to 240°C/220°C fan-forced. Oil oven tray; line with baking paper.
2 Combine oil, breadcrumbs, chilli and rind in medium bowl. Place fish on tray; pat crumb mixture onto fish. Cook about 12 minutes or until fish is cooked through.
3 Meanwhile, make crunchy nut slaw. Serve with fish.
crunchy nut slaw Combine juice, oil and sauce in large bowl. Add nuts, coriander and wombok; mix gently.
prep + cook time **25 minutes** serves **4**
nutritional count per serving **22.1g total fat (4g saturated fat); 1881kJ (450 cal); 16.2g carbohydrate; 45.3g protein; 2.7g fibre**

We used flathead fillets in this recipe.

4 x 110g white fish fillets, halved
4 turkish rolls (660g), split in half
1 baby cos lettuce (180g), leaves separated
4 hard-boiled eggs, sliced thinly
⅓ cup (25g) flaked parmesan cheese
caesar dressing
½ cup (125ml) buttermilk
1 tablespoon mayonnaise
2 teaspoons red wine vinegar
4 drained anchovy fillets, chopped finely

fish sandwiches with caesar dressing

1 Make caesar dressing.
2 Cook fish in heated oiled frying pan until cooked through. Remove from heat, cover fish; stand 5 minutes.
3 Spread roll halves with dressing; sandwich lettuce, egg, fish, cheese and remaining dressing between roll halves.
caesar dressing Combine ingredients in screw-top jar; shake well.
prep + cook time **25 minutes** makes **4**
nutritional count per roll **17.7g total fat (5.2g saturated fat); 2847kJ (681 cal); 77.5g carbohydrate; 49.2g protein; 2.3g fibre**

fish and potato stew

We used ling fillets in this recipe.

1 cup (200g) australian green lentils
2 tablespoons olive oil
1 medium red onion (170g), chopped finely
3 cloves garlic, crushed
2 medium potatoes (400g), chopped coarsely
1 litre (4 cups) chicken stock
4 sprigs fresh thyme
800g skinless white fish fillets,
    cut into 5cm pieces
4 medium silver beet leaves (320g),
    trimmed, shredded finely

1 Cook lentils in medium saucepan of boiling water 10 minutes or until tender; drain.
2 Meanwhile, heat oil in large saucepan; cook onion and garlic, stirring, until onion is soft. Add potato, stock and thyme; bring to the boil. Reduce heat; simmer, uncovered, about 10 minutes, or until potato is tender. Add lentils and fish; simmer, uncovered, about 3 minutes or until fish is cooked through.
3 Add silver beet to stew; cook, stirring, until leaves are wilted.

prep + cook time **40 minutes** serves 4
nutritional count per serving **15.8g total fat** (3.4g saturated fat); 2257kJ (540 cal); 34.8g carbohydrate; 59.1g protein; 10.3g fibre

fish chowder

We used flathead fillets in this recipe.

1 tablespoon olive oil
2 rindless shortcut bacon rashers (60g),
  chopped coarsely
1 medium brown onion (150g), chopped finely
2 stalks celery (300g), trimmed, chopped finely
2 cloves garlic, crushed
1 tablespoon plain flour
1 cup (250ml) milk, heated
600g kipfler potatoes, sliced thickly
2 cups (500ml) fish stock
1 cup (250ml) water
600g white fish fillets, cut into 3cm pieces
½ cup coarsely chopped fresh flat-leaf parsley
1 teaspoon finely grated lemon rind

1 Heat oil in large saucepan; cook bacon, stirring, until crisp. Add onion, celery and garlic; cook, stirring, until onion is soft.
2 Add flour to pan; cook, stirring, until mixture bubbles and thickens. Gradually stir in milk. Add potatoes, stock and the water; bring to the boil, stirring. Reduce heat; simmer, uncovered, 10 minutes or until potato is tender.
3 Add fish to soup; cook, stirring occasionally, until fish is cooked through.
4 Remove from heat; stir in parsley and rind.
prep + cook time 40 minutes serves 4
nutritional count per serving 12.9g total fat (4.2g saturated fat); 1714kJ (410 cal); 28.4g carbohydrate; 42g protein; 5.1g fibre

We used blue-eye fillets in this recipe.

2 tablespoons olive oil
½ teaspoon dried chilli flakes
1 cup finely shredded fresh basil leaves
4 x 200g white fish fillets, skin on
2 cloves garlic, sliced thinly
2 x 400g cans chickpeas, rinsed, drained
½ cup (125ml) chicken stock
270g jar roasted red capsicum in oil,
    drained, sliced thickly
1 medium lemon (140g)

lemon and basil fish with chickpea salad

1 Combine half the oil with chilli and a third of the basil in medium bowl. Cut 2 slits in skin of each fish fillet; add fish to oil mixture, turn to coat in mixture.

2 Cook fish, skin-side down, in heated oiled large frying pan 2 minutes; turn, cook a further 3 minutes or until cooked through. Transfer to plate; cover fish, stand 5 minutes.

3 Heat remaining oil in same pan; cook garlic, stirring, 30 seconds. Add chickpeas, stock and capsicum; simmer, uncovered, 3 minutes or until stock is almost evaporated.

4 Meanwhile, using a vegetable peeler, peel rind from lemon; slice rind thinly. Juice lemon; add 2 tablespoons of juice to chickpeas with rind. Stir in remaining basil. Serve salad with fish.

prep + cook time **25 minutes** serves **4**
nutritional count per serving **19.6g total fat** (3.4g saturated fat); 1965kJ (470 cal); 19.5g carbohydrate; 50.3g protein; 7.2g fibre

We used ling fillets in this recipe.
Basmati rice is good with this dish.
Discard the flesh of the preserved lemon,
rinse the rind, then slice it thinly.

2 tablespoons olive oil
6cm piece fresh ginger (30g), sliced thinly
1 medium brown onion (150g), sliced thinly
3 cloves garlic, sliced thinly
2 fresh long red chillies, sliced thinly

2 teaspoons ground cumin
2 teaspoons ground coriander
1 teaspoon ground turmeric
2 large tomatoes (440g), chopped coarsely
2 cups (500ml) fish stock
¼ cup (40g) dried currants
1 tablespoon honey
600g white fish fillets, cut into 5cm pieces
50g preserved lemon rind, rinsed,
   sliced thinly
⅓ cup firmly packed fresh coriander leaves

braised fish with ginger and preserved lemon

1 Heat oil in large saucepan; cook ginger,
onion, garlic and chilli, stirring, until onion
softens and browns lightly. Add spices and
tomato; cook, stirring, 2 minutes.
2 Add stock, currants and honey to pan; bring
to the boil then simmer, uncovered, 2 minutes.
Add fish; simmer; uncovered, about 12 minutes
or until fish is cooked through. Stir in lemon;
sprinkle with coriander.

prep + cook time **35 minutes** serves **4**
nutritional count per serving **13g total fat
(2.5g saturated fat); 1400kJ (335 cal);
18.3g carbohydrate; 34.2g protein; 3.4g fibre**

whole baked fish with gremolata

2.4kg cleaned whole ocean trout
3kg coarse cooking salt
4 egg whites
1.5kg baby new potatoes
4 cloves garlic, unpeeled
1 tablespoon olive oil
10 sprigs fresh lemon thyme
350g watercress, trimmed
gremolata
½ cup finely chopped fresh flat-leaf parsley
1 tablespoon finely grated lemon rind
1 tablespoon lemon juice
1 clove garlic, chopped finely

1 Preheat oven to 200°C/180°C fan-forced.
2 Pat fish dry, inside and out, with absorbent paper.
3 Combine salt and egg whites in medium bowl. Spread half the salt mixture evenly over base of large baking dish; place fish on salt mixture, cover fish completely (except for tail) with remaining salt mixture. Bake 1 hour.
4 Meanwhile, combine potatoes, garlic, oil and thyme in large shallow baking dish; place in oven on shelf below fish. Bake about 50 minutes or until potatoes are tender.
5 Make gremolata.
6 Remove fish from oven; break salt crust with heavy knife, taking care not to cut into fish. Discard salt crust; transfer fish to large serving plate. Carefully remove skin from fish; flake flesh into large pieces.
7 Divide watercress and potatoes among serving plates; top with fish, sprinkle with gremolata. Serve with lemon wedges, if you like.
gremolata Combine ingredients in small bowl.
prep + cook time **1 hour 20 minutes** serves 6
nutritional count per serving **6.7g total fat (1.5g saturated fat); 1680kJ (402 cal); 33.4g carbohydrate; 47.8g protein; 6.9g fibre**

We used whole pink snapper in this recipe, but you can use any whole white fish. Serve with warm crusty bread, if you like.

1.8kg cleaned whole snapper
1 medium lemon (140g), sliced thinly
3 medium fennel bulbs with fronds (900g)
1 large red onion (300g), sliced thinly
¼ cup (60ml) dry white wine
2 tablespoons olive oil
100g mesclun
2 green onions, sliced thinly
lemon dressing
2 tablespoons lemon juice
1 tablespoon olive oil
2 teaspoons dijon mustard
1 teaspoon caster sugar

roasted snapper with fennel

1 Preheat oven to 200°C/180°C fan-forced.
2 Pat fish dry, inside and out, with absorbent paper. Score fish four times both sides. Place lemon inside cavity.
3 Thinly slice fennel bulbs; reserve ¼ cup of the fronds.
4 Place fennel and red onion in large shallow baking dish; place fish on fennel mixture, drizzle with combined wine and oil. Roast, uncovered, about 30 minutes or until fish is cooked through.
5 Meanwhile, make lemon dressing.
6 Combine mesclun, reserved fronds and green onion with dressing in large bowl.
7 Serve fish with fennel mixture and salad.
lemon dressing Combine ingredients in screw-top jar; shake well.
prep + cook time **40 minutes** serves **6**
nutritional count per serving **11.2g total fat (2g saturated fat); 1020kJ (244 cal); 7.1g carbohydrate; 25.2g protein; 3.9g fibre**

Steamed jasmine rice is good with this dish.

4 cleaned whole baby snapper (1.2kg)
½ cup firmly packed fresh coriander leaves
½ cup firmly packed fresh basil leaves
3 shallots (75g), sliced thinly
5cm piece fresh ginger (25g), sliced thinly
3 cloves garlic, sliced thinly
1 fresh small red thai chilli, sliced thinly
2 tablespoons dark soy sauce
2 tablespoons peanut oil

chinese-style whole baby snapper

1 Preheat oven to 220°C/200°C fan-forced. Oil oven trays; line with baking paper.
2 Pat fish dry, inside and out, with absorbent paper. Score fish three times both sides. Place fish on trays. Roast, uncovered, about 20 minutes, or until fish are cooked.
3 Meanwhile, combine herbs, shallot, ginger, garlic and chilli in medium bowl.
4 Place fish on serving plates; drizzle with sauce. Heat oil in small saucepan until very hot. Top fish with herb mixture; drizzle with hot oil.

prep + cook time **30 minutes** serves **4**
nutritional count per serving **11.1g total fat (2.3g saturated fat); 857kJ (205 cal); 1.5g carbohydrate; 24.4g protein; 1g fibre**

3.5kg cleaned whole salmon
2 x 10cm sticks fresh lemon grass (40g), halved lengthways
5cm piece fresh ginger (25g), sliced thickly
4 fresh kaffir lime leaves
2 fresh small red thai chillies, halved
1 cup loosely packed fresh coriander leaves
1 clove garlic, sliced thinly
palm sugar dressing
⅓ cup (90g) grated palm sugar
2 tablespoons fish sauce
2cm piece fresh ginger (10g), grated
1 tablespoon finely chopped coriander root and stem mixture

poached salmon
with palm sugar dressing

You will need a large stainless steel fish poacher (60cm long) for this recipe.
This dish goes well with a green salad; accompany with lime wedges.

1 Pat fish dry, inside and out, with absorbent paper. Place lemon grass, ginger, half the lime leaves and two chilli halves inside fish cavity. Place fish in large fish poacher; add enough cold water to completely cover fish. Bring slowly to a gentle simmer. Remove from heat; stand, covered, 30 minutes. Lift fish from liquid; drain well.
2 Meanwhile, make palm sugar dressing.
3 Pat fish dry with absorbent paper; place onto large serving platter. To remove skin, loosen around gills and pull skin back towards the tail.
4 Finely shred remaining lime leaves and chilli halves. Top fish with combined coriander, garlic, shredded lime leaves and chilli; drizzle with dressing.
palm sugar dressing Combine ingredients in small saucepan; bring to the boil; strain. Cool.
prep + cook time **1 hour 10 minutes (+ standing)** serves **12**
nutritional count per serving **11g total fat (2.5g saturated fat);** **1058kJ (253 cal); 7.7g carbohydrate; 30.6g protein; 0.3g fibre**

500g truss cherry tomatoes
½ cup (75g) fetta-stuffed green olives,
  chopped finely
2 tablespoons finely chopped fresh
  flat-leaf parsley
2 drained anchovy fillets, chopped finely
1 clove garlic, crushed
¼ cup (60ml) olive oil

8 cleaned whole garfish (750g), butterflied
1 medium red onion (170g), sliced thinly
2 tablespoons red wine vinegar
1 cup firmly packed fresh basil leaves, torn
2 tablespoons plain flour

tapenade-stuffed garfish

1 Preheat oven to 220°C/200°C fan-forced.
2 Place tomatoes on oiled shallow oven tray;
roast about 10 minutes.
3 Meanwhile, to make tapenade, combine olives,
parsley, anchovy, garlic and one tablespoon of
the oil in medium bowl. Fill cavities of garfish
with tapenade; secure with kitchen string.
4 Combine onion and vinegar in small bowl;
stand 10 minutes. Add basil; mix gently.
5 Coat fish in flour; shake away excess. Heat
remaining oil in large frying pan; cook fish
until browned both sides and cooked through.
6 Serve fish with tomato and basil salad.
prep + cook time **40 minutes** serves **4**
nutritional count per serving **16.8g total fat
(2.6g saturated fat); 1216kJ (291 cal);
9.6g carbohydrate; 23.2g protein; 4.8g fibre**

We used whiting in this recipe.
This recipe goes well with low-fat
natural yogurt and lemon wedges.

4 cleaned whole small
  white fish (800g)
1 tablespoon lemon juice
1 teaspoon sweet paprika
1 teaspoon ground cumin
1 clove garlic, crushed

2 tablespoons olive oil
1 teaspoon cumin seeds
1 teaspoon ground coriander
½ teaspoon ground turmeric
2 x 420g cans chickpeas, rinsed, drained
⅓ cup (80ml) chicken stock
1 fresh small red thai chilli, chopped finely
3 medium tomatoes (450g), chopped coarsely
⅓ cup coarsely chopped fresh coriander leaves

fish with spiced chickpeas

1 Pat fish dry, inside and out, with absorbent
paper. Combine juice, paprika, ground cumin,
garlic and half the oil in large bowl; add fish,
turn to coat in spice mixture.
2 Cook fish on heated oiled grill plate (or grill
or barbecue) until browned both sides and
cooked through.
3 Meanwhile, dry-fry cumin seeds, ground
coriander and turmeric in medium saucepan
over heat until fragrant. Add remaining oil and
chickpeas to pan, then stock and chilli; cook,
stirring, until hot. Remove from heat; stir in
tomato and coriander leaves.
4 Serve fish with spiced chickpeas.
prep + cook time **30 minutes** serves 4
nutritional count per serving **14.4g total fat
(2.5g saturated fat); 1480kJ (354 cal);
20.7g carbohydrate; 31.5g protein; 7.8g fibre**

snapper with orange and thyme

1kg baby new potatoes, halved
2 cloves garlic, unpeeled
8 sprigs fresh thyme
2 tablespoons olive oil
4 cleaned whole baby snapper (1.2kg)
1 small orange (180g), sliced thinly
½ cup (125ml) dry white wine
4 strips orange rind
2 tablespoons orange juice
1 teaspoon caster sugar
pinch chilli flakes
2 tablespoons coarsely chopped fresh
   flat-leaf parsley

1 Preheat oven to 220°C/200°C fan-forced.
2 Boil, steam or microwave potato until tender; drain. Divide potato, garlic and thyme among two oiled large shallow oven trays; drizzle with half the oil. Roast potatoes, in oven, 20 minutes.

3 Meanwhile, pat fish dry, inside and out, with absorbent paper. Score fish three times both sides. Place orange slices inside fish cavities.
4 Remove trays from oven; set aside garlic cloves. Top potato mixture with fish; roast about 20 minutes or until fish are cooked.
5 Meanwhile, squeeze garlic from bulbs; chop finely. Combine garlic, wine, rind, juice, sugar and chilli in small saucepan; simmer, uncovered, until reduced by half. Stir in remaining oil.
6 Divide potato among serving plates; top with fish then sprinkle with parsley and drizzle with warm orange dressing.

prep + cook time **1 hour** serves **4**
nutritional count per serving **11.3g total fat (2g saturated fat); 1697kJ (406 cal); 37.9g carbohydrate; 29.8g protein; 6.1g fibre**

lime chilli fish

We used small bream in this recipe.
This dish goes well with steamed jasmine rice.

4 cleaned whole small white fish (1kg)
⅓ cup (80ml) sweet chilli sauce
2 teaspoons finely grated lime rind
2 tablespoons lime juice
10cm stick fresh lemon grass (20g),
    chopped coarsely
2 green onions, sliced thinly
1 fresh small red thai chilli, sliced thinly
1 large banana leaf
¼ cup coarsely chopped fresh coriander

1 Pat fish dry, inside and out, with absorbent paper. Score fish three times both sides.
2 Combine sauce, rind, juice, lemon grass, onion and chilli in large bowl, add fish; turn to coat fish in mixture. Cover; refrigerate 1 hour.
3 Meanwhile, trim banana leaf into four 30cm squares. Using tongs, dip one square at a time into large saucepan of boiling water; remove immediately. Rinse under cold water; pat dry with absorbent paper.
4 Place leaves on bench; place one fish on each leaf. Fold opposite corners of leaf to enclose fish; secure each parcel with kitchen string.
5 Steam parcels in large bamboo steamer, in two batches, in single layer, over wok of simmering water about 20 minutes. Serve fish sprinkled with coriander.

prep + cook time **1 hour (+ refrigeration)** serves **4**
nutritional count per serving **3.5g total fat (1g saturated fat); 681kJ (163 cal); 4.4g carbohydrate; 27.5g protein; 1.2g fibre**

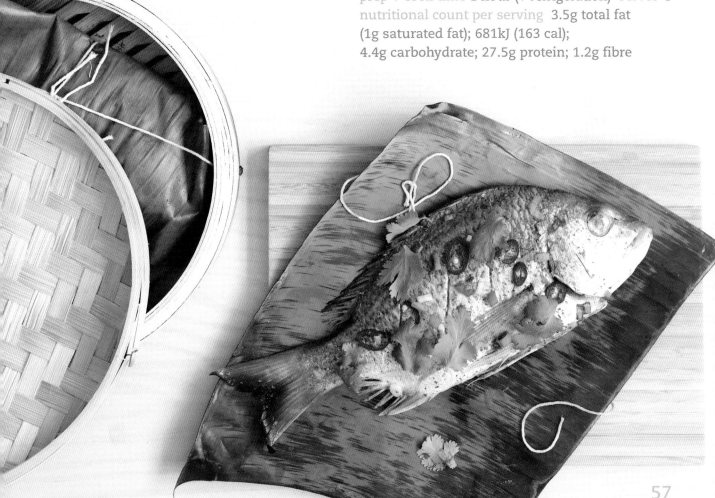

This dish goes well with a green salad.

½ medium lemon (70g), sliced thinly
8 butterflied sardines (360g)
1 fresh long red chilli, chopped finely
2 cloves garlic, crushed
lemon-infused olive oil
2 tablespoons olive oil
1 teaspoon finely grated lemon rind

chilli garlic sardines

1 Make lemon-infused olive oil.
2 Preheat oven to 220°C/200°C fan-forced.
Oil large shallow oven tray.
3 Divide lemon slices among fish cavities; tie
kitchen string around centre of fish to secure.
4 Combine half the lemon-infused olive oil
with chilli and garlic in medium bowl, add fish;
turn to coat fish in chilli mixture, place on tray.
Roast fish, uncovered, about 12 minutes or until
cooked through.
5 Serve fish drizzled with remaining lemon oil.
lemon-infused olive oil Heat oil in small
saucepan; remove from heat, add rind. Stand
10 minutes. Strain oil through fine sieve;
discard rind.
prep + cook time **35 minutes** serves **4**
nutritional count per serving 9.7g **total fat**
(1.5g saturated fat); 539kJ (129 cal);
0.4g carbohydrate; 10g protein; 0.5g fibre

This dish goes well with a green salad.

4 cleaned whole rainbow trout (1.2kg)
4 long sprigs fresh rosemary
4 slices prosciutto (60g)
1 medium lemon (140g), cut into wedges

rainbow trout with rosemary and prosciutto

1 Preheat grill.
2 Pat fish dry, inside and out, with absorbent paper. Divide rosemary among fish cavities; wrap a slice of prosciutto around each fish. Place fish on oiled shallow oven tray.
3 Grill fish about 5 minutes or until prosciutto is crisp. Turn fish; grill 5 minutes or until fish is cooked through.
4 Serve fish with lemon wedges.
prep + cook time 20 minutes serves 4
nutritional count per serving 3.3g total fat (1.1g saturated fat); 698kJ (167 cal); 0.4g carbohydrate; 33.4g protein; 0.5g fibre

prawn and fennel risotto

1kg uncooked medium king prawns
1 litre (4 cups) fish stock
1½ cups (375ml) water
1 tablespoon olive oil
2 baby fennel bulbs with fronds (260g),
    chopped finely
1 medium brown onion (150g), chopped finely
2 cloves garlic, crushed
1½ cups (300g) arborio rice
½ cup (125ml) dry white wine
½ cup coarsely chopped fresh flat-leaf parsley
¼ cup finely chopped fresh chives

fennel and lemon salad
1 baby fennel bulb with fronds (130g),
    chopped finely
2 tablespoons lemon juice
1 tablespoon olive oil

1 Shell and devein prawns. Make fennel and lemon salad.
2 Combine stock and the water in large saucepan; bring to the boil. Reduce heat; simmer, covered.
3 Heat oil in large saucepan; cook fennel, onion and garlic, stirring, until soft. Add rice; stir to coat in mixture. Add wine; cook, stirring, until liquid is almost evaporated.
4 Stir 1 cup simmering stock mixture into rice mixture; cook, stirring, over medium heat until liquid is absorbed. Continue adding stock mixture in 1-cup batches, stirring, until liquid is absorbed after each addition. Add prawns with last cup of stock mixture; cook, stirring, until prawns and rice are tender. This will take about 25 minutes in total.
5 Stir herbs into risotto. Serve risotto with fennel and lemon salad.
fennel and lemon salad Combine ingredients in medium bowl.

prep + cook time **55 minutes** serves **4**
nutritional count per serving **10.9g total fat (1.7g saturated fat); 2215kJ (530 cal); 65.3g carbohydrate; 34.9g protein; 3.4g fibre**

These pizzas are great topped with baby rocket tossed in olive oil and lemon juice.

1kg uncooked medium king prawns, shelled, deveined, halved lengthways
4 cloves garlic, crushed
1 tablespoon olive oil
2 tablespoons tomato paste
200g cherry tomatoes, halved
4 large fresh basil leaves
¼ teaspoon dried chilli flakes
1 cup coarsely torn fresh basil leaves

pizza bases
2 cups (300g) plain flour
7g dry yeast
1 teaspoon caster sugar
1 tablespoon olive oil
¾ cup (180ml) lukewarm water

garlic prawn and herb pizzas

1 Preheat oven to 240°C/220°C fan-forced. Place two oven trays in oven to heat.
2 Make pizza bases.
3 Combine prawns, garlic and oil in bowl.
4 Blend or process paste, tomato, whole basil leaves and chilli until chopped finely.
5 Place two pizza bases on heated trays; spread each with a quarter of the tomato mixture. Bake 6 minutes or until beginning to crisp. Top each with a quarter of the prawn mixture; bake about 6 minutes or until bases are crisp and prawns are cooked; sprinkle each with a quarter of the torn basil. Repeat with remaining pizza bases.
pizza bases Combine dry ingredients in large bowl; stir in oil and the water. Knead dough on floured surface about 10 minutes or until smooth. Stand, covered, in large oiled bowl 20 minutes. Divide dough into four; knead until smooth. Roll each piece into 20cm diameter pizza base.
prep + cook time **1 hour** makes **4**
nutritional count per pizza **3.4g total fat (0.5g saturated fat); 619kJ (148 cal); 17.6g carbohydrate; 10.7g protein; 1.6g fibre**

Commercially prepared red curry pastes are available in supermarkets; adjust the amount to suit your heat tolerance.
Steamed jasmine rice goes well with this dish.

1kg uncooked medium king prawns
2 tablespoons vegetable oil
3 baby eggplants (180g), cut into 2cm pieces
¼ cup (75g) thai red curry paste (*see note, left*)
1 cup (250ml) water
270ml can light coconut milk
2 tablespoons fish sauce
2 tablespoons lime juice
1 teaspoon caster sugar
½ cup loosely packed fresh coriander leaves
½ cup loosely packed thai basil leaves
4cm piece fresh ginger (20g),
    cut into matchsticks

red prawn and eggplant curry

1 Shell and devein prawns, leaving tails intact.
2 Heat oil in large frying pan; cook eggplant, stirring, until browned lightly. Add curry paste; cook, stirring, until fragrant. Stir in the water and coconut milk; bring to the boil. Reduce heat, simmer, uncovered, 3 minutes.
3 Add sauce, juice, sugar and prawns to pan; simmer, stirring, until prawns are cooked. Remove from heat, stir in half the herbs and half the ginger. Serve curry sprinkled with remaining herbs and ginger.
prep + cook time **35 minutes** serves **4**
nutritional count per serving **24g total fat (9.2g saturated fat); 1568kJ (375 cal); 8.9g carbohydrate; 29.4g protein; 3.6g fibre**

6 sheets fillo pastry
cooking-oil spray
¼ cup (60g) light sour cream
1 tablespoon lemon juice
1 tablespoon water
1 tablespoon mayonnaise
1 medium avocado (250g), chopped coarsely
150g grape tomatoes, quartered
18 cooked medium king prawns,
   shelled, deveined (810g)
1 baby cos lettuce (180g), shredded finely

prawn fillo tarts

1 Preheat oven to 200°C/180°C fan-forced.
Oil oven tray; line with baking paper.
2 Spray one pastry sheet with oil; fold in half
lengthways and in half again so you have a
strip of pastry about 7cm wide. Using an 8cm
cutter, wrap one long edge of pastry around
outside of cutter; gather pastry together under
cutter to make a tart case. Lower pastry, still
wrapped around cutter, onto tray; gently ease
cutter from pastry leaving tart case. Repeat
with remaining pastry sheets.
3 Bake cases about 10 minutes or until browned
lightly. Press centre of cases down with the
back of a spoon; lift onto wire rack to cool.
4 Meanwhile, combine sour cream, juice, the
water and mayonnaise in medium bowl; add
avocado, tomato and prawns, stir to combine.
5 Divide lettuce among tart cases, top with
prawn mixture.
prep + cook time **30 minutes** makes **6**
nutritional count per tart **12.5g total fat
(3.1g saturated fat); 928kJ (222 cal);
10g carbohydrate; 16.7g protein; 1.8g fibre**

1kg uncooked medium king prawns
125g bean thread noodles
1 tablespoon peanut oil
1 tablespoon light soy sauce
1 tablespoon fish sauce
1 tablespoon rice vinegar
2 cups (160g) bean sprouts
1 cup loosely packed vietnamese mint leaves
¼ cup (35g) crushed peanuts
1 fresh small red thai chilli, sliced thinly

lemon grass marinade
3 x 10cm sticks fresh lemon grass (30g),
    trimmed, chopped coarsely
¼ cup firmly packed fresh coriander leaves
1 tablespoon peanut oil
1 tablespoon fish sauce
1 tablespoon light soy sauce
3 cloves garlic

lemon grass prawn noodles

1 Make lemon grass marinade.
2 Shell and devein prawns, leaving tails intact. Combine prawns with marinade in medium bowl; stand 10 minutes.
3 Stand noodles in medium heatproof bowl of boiling water about 10 minutes or until softened. Drain; rinse under cold water, drain.
4 Meanwhile, combine oil, sauces and vinegar in large bowl. Add sprouts, mint, nuts, chilli and noodles; mix gently.
5 Cook prawns in heated oiled large frying pan until changed in colour. Add prawns to noodle mixture; toss gently.
lemon grass marinade Blend or process ingredients until chopped finely.
prep + cook time **25 minutes** serves **4**
nutritional count per serving **20.1g total fat (5.2g saturated fat); 1697kJ (406 cal); 19.7g carbohydrate; 33.9g protein; 6g fibre**

prawn cantinas

18 uncooked medium king prawns (810g)
2 tablespoons lemon juice
1 tablespoon olive oil
1 teaspoon sweet smoked paprika
6 baps or other small bread rolls
120g baby rocket leaves
buttermilk aïoli
⅓ cup (80ml) buttermilk
1 tablespoon mayonnaise
2 cloves garlic, crushed

1 Shell and devein prawns. Combine prawns, juice, oil and paprika in medium bowl.
2 Make buttermilk aïoli.
3 Cook prawn mixture in large frying pan, stirring, about 3 minutes.
4 Cut slits in top of rolls. Combine rocket and aïoli, divide among rolls; top with warm prawn mixture.
buttermilk aïoli Combine ingredients in small bowl.
prep + cook time **15 minutes** makes **6**
nutritional count per roll **6.1g total fat**
(**1g saturated fat**); **844kJ (202 cal)**;
18g carbohydrate; 17.8g protein; 1.6g fibre

chilli salt prawns

Serve with a watercress salad, if you like.

1kg uncooked medium king prawns
1 tablespoon olive oil
2 teaspoons sea salt flakes
½ teaspoon dried chilli flakes
1 teaspoon finely chopped fresh flat-leaf parsley
yogurt dipping sauce
1 cup (280g) yogurt
2 tablespoons mayonnaise
1 tablespoon finely grated lemon rind
1 tablespoon lemon juice

1 Preheat oven to 220°C/200°C fan-forced. Oil oven tray; line with baking paper.
2 Make yogurt dipping sauce.
3 Shell and devein prawns, leaving tails intact.
4 Combine prawns, oil, salt and chilli on tray; spread prawns into single layer. Cook prawns about 10 minutes.
5 Sprinkle parsley over sauce; serve with prawns.
yogurt dipping sauce Combine ingredients in small bowl.

prep + cook time **20 minutes** serves **4**
nutritional count per serving **10.9g total fat** (2.7g saturated fat); 991kJ (237 cal); 5.5g carbohydrate; 29.1g protein; 0.2g fibre

1 small daikon (400g) cut into matchsticks
1kg uncooked medium king prawns
1 tablespoon honey
1 tablespoon light soy sauce
2 teaspoons shichimi togarashi
1 tablespoon vegetable oil

2 tablespoons rice vinegar
2 tablespoons mirin
1 teaspoon caster sugar
500g red radishes, trimmed, cut
   into matchsticks
1½ cups firmly packed fresh coriander sprigs

shichimi-spiced prawns with radish salad

1 Soak daikon in medium bowl of iced water 10 minutes; drain.
2 Meanwhile, shell and devein prawns, leaving tails intact. Combine honey, sauce, seasoning and prawns in medium bowl.
3 Heat oil in large wok; cook prawns, in batches, until changed in colour.
4 Combine vinegar, mirin and sugar in medium bowl. Add radish, coriander and daikon; mix gently.
5 Serve spiced prawns with radish salad.
prep + cook time **30 minutes** serves **4**
nutritional count per serving **5.9g total fat (0.7g saturated fat); 961kJ (230 cal); 12.9g carbohydrate; 28g protein; 3.3g fibre**

Shichimi togarashi (also known as seven-spice mix or seven-spice blend) is a Japanese spice blend. It is available from specialist spice shops and Asian grocery stores.

Soak bamboo skewers in water for at least an hour before using to prevent them from scorching during cooking. Cut skewers to an appropriate size using scissors, if they are too long.

1kg uncooked medium king prawns
2 tablespoons finely chopped fresh coriander
2 cloves garlic, crushed
1 teaspoon ground coriander
1 teaspoon sweet smoked paprika
1 fresh long red chilli, chopped finely
2 tablespoons roasted pine nuts,
    chopped coarsely
1 tablespoon olive oil

bean salad
2 x 400g cans cannellini beans, rinsed, drained
1 fresh long red chilli, chopped finely
½ medium red onion (85g), chopped finely
½ cup coarsely chopped fresh coriander
¼ cup (60ml) lemon juice
2 tablespoons olive oil

prawn kebabs with bean salad

1 Shell and devein prawns; chop coarsely.
2 Blend or process prawn, fresh coriander, garlic, ground coriander, paprika and chilli to a paste; stir in nuts. Using wet hands, mould prawn mixture onto eight short bamboo skewers. Place on tray; cover, refrigerate 15 minutes.
3 Make bean salad.
4 Heat oil in large frying pan; cook kebabs, turning occasionally, about 5 minutes or until cooked through.
5 Serve kebabs with bean salad.
bean salad Combine ingredients in medium bowl.
prep + cook time **20 minutes**
(+ refrigeration) serves **4**
nutritional count per serving **20.4g total fat (2.4g saturated fat); 1714kJ (410 cal); 16.5g carbohydrate; 35.5g protein; 9.6g fibre**

1 large tomato (220g), chopped coarsely
½ cup coarsely chopped fresh coriander
4 cloves garlic, chopped coarsely
3cm piece fresh ginger (15g), peeled, sliced thinly
1 long green chilli, chopped coarsely
2 teaspoons garam masala
1 teaspoon ground turmeric

1 teaspoon mustard powder
2 teaspoons ground coriander
1kg uncooked medium king prawns
2 tablespoons olive oil
1 large brown onion (200g), chopped finely
12 fresh curry leaves
1½ cups (420g) skim milk yogurt
¼ cup firmly packed fresh coriander leaves

prawns with curry leaves and yogurt

1 Blend or process tomato, chopped coriander, garlic, ginger, chilli and spices until mixture forms a smooth paste.

2 Shell and devein prawns, leaving tails intact.

3 Heat half the oil in large frying pan over medium heat; cook onion and curry leaves, stirring, until onion is soft. Increase heat to high, add prawns; cook until prawns are changed in colour. Remove mixture from pan.

4 Heat remaining oil in same pan; cook paste, stirring, until fragrant. Whisk in yogurt; cook over very low heat until warmed through. Return prawn mixture to pan; cook until heated through. Sprinkle with coriander leaves.

prep + cook time **30 minutes** serves **4**
nutritional count per serving **10.3g total fat (1.5g saturated fat); 1145kJ (274 cal); 10.6g carbohydrate; 33.5g protein; 2.2g fibre**

This recipe goes well with steamed basmati rice.

500g cooked medium king prawns
1 telegraph cucumber (400g), seeded,
   cut into matchsticks
4 stalks celery (600g), trimmed,
   cut into matchsticks
1 cup (50g) snow pea sprouts, halved
1 long green chilli, seeded, chopped finely
½ cup firmly packed fresh mint leaves
½ cup firmly packed fresh coriander leaves

vietnamese dressing
2 tablespoons rice vinegar
2 tablespoons fish sauce
2 tablespoons light soy sauce
2 tablespoons lime juice
2 teaspoons sesame oil
1 teaspoon caster sugar

vietnamese cucumber and prawn salad

1 Make vietnamese dressing.
2 Shell and devein prawns; halve lengthways.
3 Place prawns, cucumber, celery, sprouts, chilli, herbs and dressing in large bowl; toss gently to combine.

vietnamese dressing Combine ingredients in screw-top jar; shake well.

prep + cook time **25 minutes** serves **4**
nutritional count per serving **3.4g total fat (0.5g saturated fat); 798kJ (191 cal); 8g carbohydrate; 29.5g protein; 4g fibre**

71

quinoa and citrus prawn salad

1½ cups (300g) quinoa
2 medium avocados (500g), chopped finely
1 lebanese cucumber (130g), peeled, seeded, chopped finely
½ cup coarsely chopped fresh flat-leaf parsley
2 fresh long red chillies, chopped finely
⅓ cup (80ml) lime juice
⅓ cup (80ml) lemon juice
2 tablespoons olive oil
1kg uncooked medium king prawns
1 teaspoon finely grated lime rind
1 teaspoon finely grated lemon rind

1 Cook quinoa in large saucepan of boiling water about 10 minutes or until tender; drain; rinse under cold water, drain.

2 Combine quinoa, avocado, cucumber, parsley and chilli in large bowl; gently stir in ¼ cup lime juice, ¼ cup lemon juice and half the oil.

3 Shell and devein prawns, leaving tails intact. Combine prawns, remaining oil and juices, and rinds in medium bowl. Cook prawn mixture in heated oiled large frying pan, stirring, until changed in colour. Add to salad; mix gently.

prep + cook time 30 minutes serves 4
nutritional count per serving 34.3g total fat
(6.2g saturated fat); 2776kJ (664 cal);
49.9g carbohydrate; 38.5g protein; 7.3g fibre

mediterranean-style prawns

This recipe is great served with risoni pasta.

1kg uncooked medium tiger prawns
2 tablespoons olive oil
8 green onions, sliced thinly
4 cloves garlic, sliced thinly
½ cup (125ml) dry white wine
700g bottle tomato pasta sauce
2 tablespoons coarsely chopped
   fresh oregano leaves

1 Shell and devein prawns, leaving tails intact.
2 Heat oil in large frying pan; cook prawns, onion and garlic, in two batches, until prawns are changed in colour. Transfer to large bowl.
3 Add wine to same heated pan; simmer until liquid is reduced by half. Add sauce; bring to the boil. Reduce heat; simmer, uncovered, about 5 minutes or until sauce is thickened.
4 Add prawn mixture and oregano to pan; stir gently until heated through.
prep + cook time **30 minutes** serves **4**
nutritional count per serving 3.1g total fat (0.4g saturated fat); 364kJ (87 cal); 5g carbohydrate; 7.8g protein; 1.1g fibre

600g uncooked medium king prawns
1 tablespoon olive oil
1 large leek (500g), chopped finely
2 stalks celery (300g), trimmed, chopped finely
1 medium brown onion (150g), chopped finely
2 cloves garlic, crushed

400g can cannellini beans, rinsed, drained
2 litres (8 cups) salt-reduced chicken stock
½ cup (80g) macaroni pasta
½ cup coarsely chopped fresh flat-leaf parsley

prawn and white bean soup

1 Shell and devein prawns; chop coarsely.
2 Heat oil in large saucepan; cook leek, celery, onion and garlic, stirring, until onion is soft. Add beans and stock to pan; bring to the boil. Add pasta; reduce heat, simmer, covered, about 10 minutes or until pasta is tender.
3 Add prawns to soup; simmer, uncovered, about 3 minutes or until prawns are tender. Stir in half the parsley.
4 Divide soup among serving bowls; sprinkle with remaining parsley.

prep + cook time **35 minutes** serves **6**
nutritional count per serving **5.4g total fat (1.2g saturated fat); 920kJ (220 cal); 20g carbohydrate; 19.9g protein; 6.1g fibre**

6 dried shiitake mushrooms
10g arame seaweed
360g uncooked medium king prawns
200g dried udon noodles
15g dashi powder
1.5 litres (6 cups) boiling water
½ cup (150g) white miso paste
2 x 160g skinless snapper fillets,
   cut into 1.5cm pieces
250g silken firm tofu, cut into 1cm pieces
2 green onions, cut into 2cm lengths

prawn and snapper miso soup

1 Soak mushrooms in boiling water 20 minutes; drain. Discard stems; slice caps thinly.
2 Meanwhile, soak seaweed in boiling water 5 minutes, drain.
3 Shell and devein prawns; chop coarsely.
4 Cook noodles in large saucepan of boiling water until tender; drain.
5 Meanwhile, combine dashi and the boiling water in large saucepan; bring to the boil. Place paste in small bowl; whisk in 1 cup of hot dashi stock. Add paste mixture to dashi stock in pan; whisk until combined. Bring to the boil; add prawns and snapper and simmer until seafood is cooked through.
6 Divide noodles among six serving bowls, add mushrooms, seaweed, tofu and onion; ladle over miso broth.

prep + cook time **30 minutes**
(+ standing) serves 6
nutritional count per serving **5.8g total fat
(1.1g saturated fat); 1237kJ (296 cal);
29.2g carbohydrate; 29g protein; 4.2g fibre**

balmain bug salad

Balmain bugs are a type of crayfish also known as slipper, shovelnose or southern bay lobster. Substitute balmain bugs with king prawns, lobster, scampi or moreton bay bugs, if you prefer.

150g thick rice stick noodles
8 uncooked shelled balmain bug tails (650g)
2 cloves garlic, crushed
1 tablespoon finely chopped fresh coriander
2 tablespoons vegetable oil
½ medium green papaya (500g),
 grated coarsely
2 fresh long red chillies, chopped finely
1 tablespoon fish sauce
⅓ cup (80ml) lime juice
⅔ cup loosely packed fresh coriander leaves

1 Place noodles in medium heatproof bowl, cover with boiling water; stand 20 minutes. Drain.
2 Meanwhile, combine bug tails, garlic, chopped coriander and half the oil in large bowl; cook in large heated frying pan until tails are changed in colour.
3 Combine remaining ingredients with noodles in large bowl; add warm bug tails, mix gently.

prep + cook time **30 minutes** serves **4**
nutritional count per serving **10.7g total fat (1.4g saturated fat); 1200kJ (287 cal); 15g carbohydrate; 31g protein; 2.8g fibre**

600g cuttlefish hoods
2 tablespoons olive oil
1 medium red onion (170g), sliced thinly
2 cloves garlic, sliced thinly
1½ cups (300g) arborio rice
1 tablespoon tomato paste
1 teaspoon sweet paprika
pinch saffron threads
½ cup (125ml) dry white wine

1 litre (4 cups) chicken stock
1 cup (250ml) water
4 medium tomatoes (600g), seeded,
  sliced thickly
½ cup coarsely chopped fresh
  flat-leaf parsley

cuttlefish with saffron rice

1 Cut cuttlefish down centre to open out. Score inside in a diagonal pattern. Cut cuttlefish, lengthways, into three pieces.
2 Heat half the oil in large deep frying pan; cook onion and garlic, stirring, until onion is soft. Stir in rice, paste, paprika and saffron. Add wine; cook, stirring, until liquid is almost evaporated. Stir in stock and the water; bring to the boil, then simmer, uncovered, until rice is tender and liquid is almost evaporated.
3 Meanwhile, heat remaining oil in large frying pan; cook cuttlefish, stirring, until cuttlefish changes colour. Remove from heat, stir in tomato and parsley.
4 Serve saffron rice topped with cuttlefish mixture. Serve with lemon wedges, if you like.
prep + cook time **30 minutes** serves **4**
nutritional count per serving **12.6g total fat (2.5g saturated fat); 2316kJ (554 cal); 67g carbohydrate; 35.4g protein; 3.8g fibre**

2 cups (500ml) fish stock
1 cup (250ml) water
⅓ cup (80ml) lime juice
2 tablespoons fish sauce
1 tablespoon vegetable oil
½ medium green papaya (500g),
    cut into matchsticks

½ small pineapple (450g),
    sliced thinly lengthways
1 cup loosely packed fresh coriander sprigs
2 fresh long red chillies, sliced thinly
¼ cup (35g) coarsely chopped unsalted
    roasted pistachios
800g baby squid hoods, sliced thinly

squid and green papaya salad

1 Combine stock and the water in large
saucepan; bring to the boil.
2 Meanwhile, combine juice, sauce and oil in
large bowl; add papaya, pineapple, coriander,
chilli and nuts, mix gently to combine.
3 Add squid to stock mixture; cook until
squid is changed in colour; drain. Add hot
squid to salad mixture and toss to combine.
Serve immediately.
prep + cook time **30 minutes** serves **4**
nutritional count per serving **11.9g total fat
(2g saturated fat); 1371kJ (328 cal);
13.9g carbohydrate; 38.8g protein; 4.5g fibre**

We used flathead fillets for this recipe.
You need to soak 24 bamboo skewers in water
for at least an hour before using to prevent them
from scorching during cooking.

8 cuttlefish hoods (920g)
8 uncooked medium king prawns (360g)
4 white fish fillets (440g), halved lengthways
½ cup loosely packed fresh mint leaves
½ cup loosely packed fresh coriander leaves
1 cup (80g) bean sprouts
40g baby asian salad greens

chilli dressing
2 long green chillies, chopped finely
2 teaspoons caster sugar
¼ cup (60ml) lime juice
2 tablespoons fish sauce
2 cloves garlic, crushed
2 tablespoons vegetable oil
1 tablespoon finely chopped fresh coriander

seafood kebabs

1 Cut cuttlefish hoods down one long side
to open out. Score inside of hood in diagonal
pattern; fold hood in half with scored-side facing
out. Thread lengthways onto eight skewers.
2 Shell and devein prawns, leaving tails intact.
Thread lengthways onto eight skewers.
3 Thread fish, lengthways, onto eight skewers.
4 Make chilli dressing.
5 Combine herbs, sprouts and asian greens
in medium bowl; drizzle with a quarter of
the dressing.
6 Place kebabs on oven tray; pour remaining
dressing over kebabs, turn to coat in dressing.
Cook kebabs on heated oiled grill plate (or grill
or barbecue) until seafood is cooked through.
7 Serve kebabs with salad.
chilli dressing Combine ingredients in
screw-top jar; shake well.
prep + cook time **30 minutes** serves **4**
nutritional count per serving **13.6g total fat**
(2.6g saturated fat); 1827kJ (437 cal);
4g carbohydrate; 73.1g protein; 1.9g fibre

Serve with a watercress salad, if you like.

500g potatoes, chopped coarsely
2 egg whites
250g cooked crab meat
4 green onions, chopped finely
¼ cup coarsely chopped fresh flat-leaf parsley
2 tablespoons self-raising flour
1 cup (70g) stale sourdough breadcrumbs
cooking-oil spray

tzatziki
2 lebanese cucumbers (260g), halved, seeded
2 cloves garlic, crushed
1 teaspoon lemon juice
1 cup (280g) yogurt

crab cakes with tzatziki

1 Oil oven tray; line with baking paper.
2 Boil, steam or microwave potato until tender; drain. Mash potato in large bowl until smooth; cool.
3 Whisk egg whites in small bowl until frothy; add to potato with crab, onion, parsley and flour. Shape mixture into eight patties; place on tray. Cover; refrigerate 10 minutes.
4 Meanwhile, preheat oven to 220°C/200°C fan-forced.
5 Make tzatziki.
6 Coat patties in breadcrumbs, spray with a little oil; return to tray. Bake about 30 minutes or until browned lightly. Serve with tzatziki.
tzatziki Coarsely grate cucumbers; squeeze out excess moisture. Place in large bowl with garlic, juice and yogurt; stir to combine.
prep + cook time 45 minutes serves 4
nutritional count per serving 4.5g total fat (1.8g saturated fat); 1032kJ (247 cal); 31.2g carbohydrate; 18g protein; 4g fibre

stir-fried salt and pepper squid

Serve with some rocket leaves and lemon cheeks.

1kg squid hoods
½ cup (75g) cornflour
2 teaspoons sea salt flakes
2 teaspoons finely grated lemon rind
2 teaspoons freshly ground peppercorn medley
2 tablespoons vegetable oil

1 Cut squid down centre to open out; score inside in a diagonal pattern. Halve squid lengthways; cut into 5cm pieces.
2 Combine squid, cornflour, salt, rind and pepper in large bowl.
3 Heat oil in large wok; stir-fry squid, in batches, until tender and golden.

prep + cook time **30 minutes** serves **4**
nutritional count per serving **12.3g total fat**
(2.2g saturated fat); 1430kJ (342 cal);
15.7g carbohydrate; 41.8g protein; 0.1g fibre

Peppercorn medley is a mix of black, white, green and pink peppercorns, coriander seeds and allspice. It is sold in disposable grinders in supermarkets.

spicy calamari with olives

2 tablespoons olive oil
1 medium red onion (170g), chopped finely
3 cloves garlic, crushed
2 fresh small red thai chillies, sliced thinly
½ cup (125ml) dry white wine
2 x 400g cans cherry tomatoes
¾ cup (180ml) water
800g baby calamari with tentacles
1 cup (160g) sicilian green olives, seeded
½ cup firmly packed fresh basil leaves
2 teaspoons finely grated lemon rind
8 slices (280g) ciabatta bread, toasted

1 Heat oil in large saucepan; cook onion, garlic and chilli, stirring, until onion is soft. Add wine; bring to the boil. Reduce heat; simmer until liquid is reduced by half.
2 Add undrained tomatoes and the water to pan; bring to the boil. Reduce heat; simmer 15 minutes or until mixture is thickened slightly.
3 Add calamari, olives and half the basil to pan; cook about 3 minutes or until calamari is tender.
4 Remove from heat; stir in remaining basil and rind. Serve calamari with toasted ciabatta.

prep + cook time **30 minutes** serves **4**
nutritional count per serving **14.3g total fat (2.5g saturated fat); 2211kJ (529 cal); 49.3g carbohydrate; 42g protein; 6.1g fibre**

4 medium potatoes (800g), chopped coarsely
2 small uncooked lobster tails in the shells (330g)
1 tablespoon olive oil
1 teaspoon finely grated lemon rind
4 medium tomatoes (600g), peeled,
   seeded, chopped coarsely
1 cup firmly packed fresh basil leaves

vinaigrette
2 tablespoons olive oil
2 tablespoons red wine vinegar
1 tablespoon dijon mustard
1 tablespoon warm water

lobster with tomato, potato and basil salad

1 Boil, steam or microwave potato until tender; drain. Cool.
2 Meanwhile, make vinaigrette.
3 Remove lobster meat from shells; cut meat crossways into medallions about 2cm thick. Combine lobster, oil and rind in medium bowl. Cook lobster, in heated oiled large frypan, about 2 minutes each side or until cooked through.
4 Combine tomato, basil, potato and lobster in large bowl; drizzle with vinaigrette.
vinaigrette Combine ingredients in screw-top jar; shake well.
prep + cook time **30 minutes** serves **4**
nutritional count per serving **14.7g total fat (2.1g saturated fat); 1363kJ (326 cal); 25.4g carbohydrate; 20.6g protein; 4.9g fibre**

800g squid hoods
200g swiss brown mushrooms, halved
2½ tablespoons korean chilli paste (gochoojang)
2 cloves garlic, crushed
3 green onions, sliced thinly
2 tablespoons light soy sauce
1 teaspoon sesame oil
1 teaspoon caster sugar

cucumber salad
1 telegraph cucumber (400g),
   cut into matchsticks
1 small carrot (70g), cut into matchsticks
3 green onions, sliced thinly
1 tablespoon sesame seeds, toasted
¼ teaspoon dried chilli flakes
¼ cup (60ml) white wine vinegar

barbecued squid and cucumber salad

1 Cut squid down centre to open out; score the inside in a diagonal pattern. Halve squid lengthways; cut into 5cm pieces. Combine in medium bowl with remaining ingredients.
2 Make cucumber salad.
3 Cook squid mixture on heated oiled grill plate (or grill or barbecue), in batches, until tender. Combine squid mixture with cucumber salad.
cucumber salad Combine cucumber, carrot, onion, seeds and chilli in medium bowl. Add vinegar; stand 5 minutes then toss gently.
prep + cook time 30 minutes serves 4
nutritional count per serving 5.5g total fat (1.2g saturated fat); 978kJ (234 cal); 6.1g carbohydrate; 37.2g protein; 4.9g fibre

Korean chilli paste is a very hot chilli paste available from many Asian grocery stores.

We used ling fillets in this recipe.
Pot-ready mussels come in 1kg bags. They have been scrubbed and bearded and are ready to cook.

500g pipis, rinsed, drained
1 tablespoon olive oil
2 stalks celery (300g), trimmed, chopped finely
1 medium brown onion (150g), chopped finely
3 cloves garlic, bruised
½ cup (125ml) dry white wine

1kg pot-ready black mussels
375g fettuccine pasta
pinch saffron threads
1½ tablespoons cornflour
¼ cup (60ml) water
200g white fish fillets, chopped coarsely
8 uncooked medium king prawns (360g),
    shelled, deveined, chopped coarsely
¼ cup coarsely chopped fresh flat-leaf parsley

shellfish pasta

1 Place pipis in large bowl; cover with cold water. Stand 15 minutes; rinse well then drain.
2 Heat oil in large saucepan; cook celery, onion and garlic, stirring, until onion is soft. Add wine; bring to the boil. Add mussels and pipis; cook, covered, about 3 minutes or until shells open (discard any that do not). Strain through a colander over medium bowl; reserve stock.
3 Remove mussels from shells; place mussels in medium bowl with pipis. Strain reserved stock through a fine sieve into large saucepan.
4 Meanwhile, cook pasta in large saucepan of boiling water until tender; drain.
5 Boil stock then stir in saffron and blended cornflour and the water; boil until stock thickens slightly. Add fish and prawns; cook until prawns change colour. Add pasta and remaining seafood.
6 Serve shellfish pasta sprinkled with parsley.

prep + cook time **30 minutes**
(+ standing) serves **4**
nutritional count per serving **7.3g total fat
(1.2g saturated fat); 2328kJ (557 cal);
72.9g carbohydrate; 41g protein; 5.1g fibre**

We used carnaroli risotto rice for this recipe as it holds its shape very well. If you can't find it, or it's not available, use arborio rice.
A large wok lid makes a good cover for the pan.

8 uncooked medium king prawns (360g)
400g medium black mussels
2 tablespoons olive oil
2 chicken thigh fillets (400g), chopped coarsely
1 medium red onion (170g), chopped finely
2 cloves garlic, crushed
1 teaspoon sweet paprika
pinch saffron threads
1½ cups (300g) white short-grain rice
1 litre (4 cups) chicken stock
4 baby squid hoods (360g), sliced thinly
2 medium tomatoes (300g), seeded, chopped finely
½ cup coarsely chopped fresh flat-leaf parsley

paella

1 Shell and devein prawns, leaving tails intact. Scrub mussels; remove beards.
2 Heat half the oil in large deep frying pan or 46cm paella pan; cook chicken until browned. Remove from pan. Heat remaining oil in same pan; cook onion, garlic, paprika and saffron, stirring, until onion softens. Stir in rice.
3 Add stock to pan; bring to the boil, stirring. Reduce heat; simmer, uncovered, about 12 minutes or until rice is almost tender. Stir in chicken; cook 3 minutes.
4 Scatter prawns, mussels and squid evenly over rice mixture, cover with a domed lid or foil; simmer about 5 minutes, stirring once, or until prawns are cooked and mussels have opened (discard any that do not). Remove paella from heat, scatter with tomato and parsley. Stand, covered, 5 minutes before serving.
prep + cook time **30 minutes** serves **4**
nutritional count per serving **19.6g total fat (4.6g saturated fat); 2784kJ (666 cal); 65.9g carbohydrate; 54.9g protein; 2.7g fibre**

oysters with pickled lemon

You need a thin-skinned lemon for this recipe.
We used a meyer lemon.

1 medium lemon (140g)
2 tablespoons white wine vinegar
2 tablespoons olive oil
2 shallots (50g), chopped finely
2 tablespoons finely chopped chives
24 rock oysters, on the half shell

1 Halve lemon lengthways, cut each half into 1cm wedges, slice thinly crossways.
2 Combine lemon, vinegar, oil, shallot and chives in small bowl; stand 10 minutes.
3 Top oysters with pickled lemon mixture. Serve immediately.

prep time 10 minutes serves 4
nutritional count per serving 10.6g total fat (1.8g saturated fat); 556kJ (133 cal); 1.4g carbohydrate; 7.7g protein; 1g fibre

mussels with tomato and chilli

Pot-ready mussels come in 1kg bags. They have been scrubbed and bearded and are ready to cook.

1 tablespoon olive oil
4 shallots (100g), sliced thinly
4 cloves garlic, sliced thinly
3 fresh long red chillies, sliced thinly
    lengthways
1 cup (250ml) dry white wine
2 x 400g cans cherry tomatoes
2kg pot-ready black mussels
½ cup coarsely chopped fresh flat-leaf parsley

1 Heat oil in large saucepan; cook shallot, garlic and chilli, stirring, until fragrant.
2 Stir in wine and undrained tomatoes; bring to the boil. Add mussels; cook, covered, 3 minutes or until mussels open (discard any that do not). Stir in parsley.

prep + cook time 25 minutes serves 4
nutritional count per serving 6.9g total fat
(1.2g saturated fat); 899kJ (215 cal);
12.2g carbohydrate; 14.3g protein; 3.5g fibre

16 uncooked medium king prawns (720g)
600g white fish fillets
16 scallops (400g) without roe
⅓ cup (95g) hoisin sauce
2 tablespoons light soy sauce
1 tablespoon fish sauce
2 tablespoons rice vinegar
2 cups (160g) bean sprouts
1 medium red capsicum (200g), sliced thinly
1 medium green capsicum (200g), sliced thinly
4 green onions, sliced thinly
½ cup firmly packed fresh coriander leaves
5cm piece fresh ginger (25g),
   cut into matchsticks

hoisin seafood skewers with ginger salad

We used ling fillets in this recipe, but you can use your favourite white fish fillet.
You need to soak eight bamboo skewers in cold water for at least an hour to prevent them from scorching during cooking. Serve the skewers with lime wedges, if you like.

1 Preheat oven to 240°C/220°C fan-forced. Oil oven tray; line with baking paper.
2 Shell and devein prawns, leaving tails intact. Cut fish into 16 pieces. Thread seafood, alternately, onto eight skewers; place on tray.
3 Combine sauces in small jug, drizzle half the sauce mixture over skewers; turn to coat in sauce. Roast skewers about 10 minutes, or until seafood is cooked through.
4 Combine remaining sauce mixture, vinegar, sprouts, capsicums, onion, coriander and ginger in large bowl; toss to combine.
5 Serve seafood skewers with salad.

prep + cook time **30 minutes** serves **4**

nutritional count per serving **2.8g total fat (0.5g saturated fat); 1116kJ (267 cal); 13.8g carbohydrate; 43.3g protein; 5.1g fibre**

hot-smoked trout salad

200g bean thread noodles
400g hot-smoked trout fillets
2 lebanese cucumbers (260g), seeded,
  sliced thinly
¼ cup (35g) pistachios, roasted
½ cup firmly packed fresh mint leaves
⅓ cup firmly packed thai basil leaves
chilli, lime and sesame dressing
1 fresh long red chilli, chopped finely
1 clove garlic, crushed
⅓ cup (80ml) lime juice
1 tablespoon sesame oil
2 tablespoons fish sauce

1 Place noodles in large heatproof bowl, cover
with boiling water; stand until almost tender,
drain. Rinse under cold water; drain.
2 Make chilli, lime and sesame dressing.
3 Discard skin and bones from fish. Flake fish
into large pieces; add to noodles in large bowl
with cucumber, nuts and herbs.
4 Divide salad among serving bowls; drizzle
with dressing.
chilli, lime and sesame dressing Combine
ingredients in screw-top jar; shake well.
prep + cook time **25 minutes** serves **4**
nutritional count per serving **14.2g total fat**
(2.3g saturated fat); 1300kJ (311 cal);
14.7g carbohydrate; 29.6g protein; 2.7g fibre

To roast nuts, place shelled nuts on a baking tray
and bake in a moderate oven, stirring occasionally,
until they're browned lightly, about 10 minutes.

375g fettuccine pasta
1 tablespoon olive oil
2 shallots, chopped finely
2 cloves garlic, crushed
¼ cup (60ml) lemon juice
1 tablespoon coarsely chopped fresh tarragon
1 tablespoon coarsely chopped fresh dill
1 tablespoon coarsely chopped fresh chervil
200g smoked salmon slices, chopped coarsely

salmon and herb pasta

1 Cook pasta in large saucepan of boiling water, uncovered, until tender; drain, reserving ¼ cup cooking liquid.
2 Meanwhile, heat oil in small saucepan; cook shallot and garlic, stirring; until shallot softens.
3 Return pasta to pan with reserved cooking liquid, shallot mixture and remaining ingredients; mix gently.

prep + cook time **25 minutes** serves **4**
nutritional count per serving 7.7g **total fat** (1.2g saturated fat); 1450kJ (347 cal); 47.8g carbohydrate; 19.6g protein; 2.8g fibre

This dish goes well with a rocket salad.

210g smoked kipper fillets
375g thin spaghetti
30g butter
2 tablespoons plain flour
2 cups (500ml) warm skim milk
2 tablespoons finely chopped fresh
   flat-leaf parsley
2 tablespoons rinsed, drained capers,
   chopped coarsely
2 tablespoons finely grated parmesan cheese
2 teaspoons dijon mustard

herbed kipper pasta

1 Preheat grill.
2 Place fish, skin-side down, on oiled oven tray; grill about 4 minutes or until heated through. Cool 10 minutes. Discard skin and bones from fish; flake fish into small pieces.
3 Cook pasta in large saucepan of boiling water until tender; drain.
4 Meanwhile, melt butter in medium saucepan, add flour; cook, stirring, until mixture bubbles and thickens slightly. Gradually add milk, stirring, until mixture boils and thickens. Stir in parsley, capers, cheese and mustard.
5 Combine sauce with fish and pasta in large bowl.

prep + cook time **25 minutes** serves **4**
nutritional count per serving **11.2g total fat (5.7g saturated fat); 2236kJ (535 cal); 75.2g carbohydrate; 30.4g protein; 3.6g fibre**

1½ cups (375ml) fish stock
1 cup (250ml) water
2 sprigs fresh thyme
1 bay leaf
6 black peppercorns
300g salmon fillets, cut into 3cm pieces
300g smoked cod fillets, cut into 3cm pieces
300g snapper fillets, cut into 3cm pieces
4 large potatoes (1.2kg), chopped coarsely
¼ cup (60ml) milk
60g butter
¼ cup (35g) plain flour
2 tablespoons coarsely chopped fresh chervil
2 tablespoons coarsely chopped fresh chives

fish pie

The fish pie goes well with steamed baby green beans.

1 Combine stock, the water, thyme, bay leaf and peppercorns in large saucepan; bring to the boil. Add fish, reduce heat; simmer gently, uncovered, about 2 minutes or until cooked through. Using a slotted spoon, remove fish from pan; divide fish among four 1½-cup (375ml) ovenproof dishes. Strain liquid through sieve into large heatproof jug. Discard solids; reserve stock.

2 Boil, steam or microwave potato until tender; drain. Push potato through sieve into large bowl; add milk and half the butter, stir until smooth. Cover to keep warm.

3 Preheat grill.

4 Melt remaining butter in medium saucepan, add flour; cook, stirring, until mixture bubbles and thickens slightly. Gradually stir in reserved stock; cook, stirring, until mixture boils and thickens. Stir in herbs.

5 Divide sauce among dishes; cover each with potato mixture. Place on oven tray; grill until browned lightly.

prep + cook time **45 minutes** serves **4**
nutritional count per serving **20.7g total fat (10.5g saturated fat); 2353kJ (563 cal); 39.2g carbohydrate; 52.4g protein; 4.3g fibre**

This dish goes well with a rocket salad.

2 medium potatoes (400g), chopped coarsely
175 asparagus, trimmed
2 tablespoons coarsely chopped fresh chives
150g sliced smoked trout
4 eggs
2 egg whites
½ cup (125ml) milk

smoked trout frittata

1 Preheat oven to 180°C/160°C fan-forced.
Oil and line deep 19cm-square cake pan.
2 Boil, steam or microwave potatoes and
asparagus, separately, until tender; drain.
Place in prepared pan with chives, top
with trout.
3 Whisk eggs, egg whites and milk together
in large jug; pour into pan. Bake, uncovered, in
oven, about 40 minutes or until frittata is set.
4 Stand frittata 5 minutes before cutting.
prep + cook time **55 minutes** serves **4**
nutritional count per serving **8.5g total fat
(2.9g saturated fat); 924kJ (221 cal);
13.3g carbohydrate; 21.7g protein; 1.9g fibre**

800g medium potatoes, unpeeled, washed
⅓ cup (80ml) buttermilk
1 tablespoon prepared horseradish
1 tablespoon finely chopped fresh
   flat-leaf parsley
2 tablespoons olive oil
100g smoked salmon slices
40g baby rocket leaves

smoked salmon rösti stacks

1 Boil, steam or microwave whole potatoes
5 minutes; drain. Cool 20 minutes.
2 Meanwhile, combine buttermilk, horseradish
and parsley in small bowl.
3 Coarsely grate potatoes into medium bowl.
4 Heat oil in large frying pan; drop ¼ cups
grated potato into pan, flatten with spatula.
Cook rösti, in batches, until browned both sides.
5 Layer rösti with salmon and rocket; serve
with buttermilk dressing.
prep + cook time 40 minutes
(+ cooling) serves 4
nutritional count per serving 11.5g total fat
(2.1g saturated fat); 1141kJ (273 cal);
28.3g carbohydrate; 11.8g protein; 4.3g fibre

smoked trout tarts

cooking-oil spray
6 sheets fillo pastry
1 whole smoked trout (240g), skinned, flaked
½ cup (60g) frozen peas
3 eggs
¼ cup (60ml) skim milk
2 tablespoons light sour cream
1 tablespoon coarsely chopped fresh dill

1 Preheat oven to 200°C/180°C fan-forced.
Oil six 10cm round loose-based flan tins.
2 Lightly spray one pastry sheet with oil spray;
fold into a square, then fold into quarters to form
a smaller square. Repeat with remaining pastry.
Line tins with pastry, press into sides.
3 Divide trout and peas among pastry cases.
4 Whisk eggs, milk, cream and dill in medium
jug. Pour equal amounts into pastry cases.
5 Bake tarts about 20 minutes or until filling sets.
Cool 10 minutes before serving.

prep + cook time **40 minutes** makes 6
nutritional count per tart **8.7g total fat**
(3.2g saturated fat); 748kJ (179 cal);
9g carbohydrate; 15.9g protein; 1g fibre

smoked cod with parsley butter

This dish goes well with creamy mashed potato and steamed sugar snap peas.

4 x 120g smoked cod fillets
40g butter, softened
1 tablespoon finely chopped fresh
   flat-leaf parsley

1 Place fish in large deep frying pan; cover with cold water. Bring slowly to a gentle simmer, uncovered. Remove from heat; drain. Repeat process once more; drain.
2 Combine butter and parsley in small bowl.
3 Preheat grill.
4 Divide fish among four 1½ cup (375ml) shallow ovenproof dishes; dollop with parsley butter. Stand dishes on oven tray; grill until butter melts.

prep + cook time **35 minutes** serves **4**
nutritional count per serving **9.4g total fat** (5.8g saturated fat); 736kJ (176 cal); 0.1g carbohydrate; 22.6g protein; 0.1g fibre

500g cherry tomatoes
2 teaspoons olive oil
250g rocket leaves, trimmed
1 lebanese cucumber (130g),
    seeded, sliced thinly
200g smoked salmon slices, chopped coarsely

dill dressing
2 tablespoons lemon juice
1 tablespoon olive oil
1 tablespoon coarsely chopped fresh dill
2 teaspoons wholegrain mustard
1 teaspoon caster sugar

smoked salmon and cherry tomato salad

1 Preheat oven to 200°C/180°C fan-forced.
2 Combine tomatoes and oil in medium shallow baking dish. Roast about 10 minutes or until tomatoes split.
3 Meanwhile, make dill dressing.
4 Combine tomatoes with remaining ingredients and dressing in large bowl.
dill dressing Combine ingredients in screw-top jar; shake well.
prep + cook time **20 minutes** serves **4**
nutritional count per serving **9.7g total fat** (1.4g saturated fat); 706kJ (169 cal); 5.7g carbohydrate; 13.6g protein; 3.1g fibre

We used butter beans in this recipe, but any canned white beans will do.

240g whole smoked trout
¼ cup (60ml) lemon juice
2 tablespoons olive oil
1 tablespoon wholegrain mustard
2 teaspoons honey
420g can rinsed, drained white beans
350g watercress, trimmed
½ cup coarsely chopped fresh flat-leaf parsley
¼ cup (45g) drained cornichons

smoked trout and white bean salad

1 Discard skin and bones from fish; flake fish into large bowl.
2 Combine juice, oil, mustard and honey in screw-top jar; shake well.
3 Add remaining ingredients and dressing to bowl with fish; mix gently.

prep + cook time 20 minutes serves 4
nutritional count per serving 11.2g total fat (1.7g saturated fat); 924kJ (221 cal); 14.1g carbohydrate; 13.4g protein; 5.7g fibre

sweet potato and salmon patties

2 large potatoes (600g), chopped coarsely
1 medium kumara (400g), chopped coarsely
20g butter
415g can pink salmon, drained, flaked
1 egg yolk
2 tablespoons finely chopped fresh chervil
1 tablespoon finely chopped fresh chives
1 cup (70g) stale breadcrumbs

1 Boil, steam or microwave potato and kumara until tender; drain. Mash potato and kumara with butter in medium bowl until almost smooth. Cool 20 minutes.
2 Stir salmon, egg yolk and herbs into potato mixture. Shape mixture into eight patties. Cover; refrigerate 1 hour.
3 Preheat oven to 200°C/180°C fan-forced. Oil oven tray; line with baking paper.
4 Coat patties in breadcrumbs; place on tray. Bake about 40 minutes or until browned lightly. Serve with a rocket salad and lemon wedges, if you like.

prep + cook time 55 minutes
(+ cooling and refrigeration) makes 8
nutritional count per pattie 6.2g total fat
(2.3g saturated fat); 798kJ (191 cal);
20.4g carbohydrate; 12.2g protein; 2.2g fibre

angel hair pasta with tomato, tuna and capers

Cook 300g angel hair pasta in large saucepan of boiling water until tender; drain. Transfer pasta to large bowl. Meanwhile, drain 425g can tuna in oil over small bowl; reserve 2 tablespoons of the oil. Flake tuna. Add 4 finely chopped medium tomatoes, 2 tablespoons rinsed, drained baby capers, ¼ cup coarsely chopped fresh flat-leaf parsley, tuna and reserved oil to pasta; mix gently.

prep + cook time **20 minutes** serves **4**
nutritional count per serving **22.3g total fat
(3g saturated fat); 2312kJ (553 cal);
54.6g carbohydrate; 31g protein; 4.6g fibre**

Angel hair pasta, also known as barbina, or "capelli d'angelo" in Italian, are long, delicate strands of spaghetti-like pasta.

tuna rice cake

Heat 2 teaspoons of olive oil in a deep 20cm frying pan; cook 1 finely chopped brown onion and 2 crushed garlic cloves until onion softens. Combine onion mixture with 2 cups cooked white medium-grain rice, 425g can drained flaked tuna in spring water, 310g can rinsed, drained corn kernels, 4 thinly sliced green onions and 3 beaten eggs in a large bowl. Heat same pan; add rice mixture, press down gently. Sprinkle with ½ cup coarsely grated gouda cheese. Cook, covered, 10 minutes. Preheat grill; grill about 10 minutes or until browned lightly.

prep + cook time **35 minutes** serves **6**
nutritional count per serving **9.4g total fat
(3.6g saturated fat); 1271kJ (304 cal);
29.4g carbohydrate; 23.7g protein; 2.8g fibre**

The rice cake goes well with a green salad.

tuna and basil salad

Combine 1 thinly sliced medium red onion and ¼ cup
red wine vinegar in large bowl; stand 10 minutes.
Meanwhile, drain 425g can tuna in oil over small bowl;
reserve 2 tablespoons of the oil. Flake tuna. Add 420g can
rinsed, drained cannellini beans, 2 tablespoons rinsed,
drained baby capers, 2 finely chopped seeded medium
tomatoes, flaked tuna and the reserved oil to onion
mixture; mix gently. Divide 100g baby rocket leaves
among serving plates; top with tuna mixture, sprinkle
with ¼ cup baby basil leaves.
prep + cook time **15 minutes** serves **4**
nutritional count per serving **22g total fat**
(2.8g saturated fat); 1526kJ (365 cal);
11.9g carbohydrate; 27.1g protein; 6.2g fibre

rollini arrabiata with tuna

Heat 2 teaspoons olive oil in medium saucepan; cook
1 finely chopped brown onion, 3 crushed garlic cloves
and 2 finely chopped fresh long red chillies, stirring,
until onion softens. Add 700g jar bottled tomato pasta
sauce; bring to the boil. Reduce heat; simmer, uncovered,
about 25 minutes or until sauce thickens slightly. Stir
in 425g can drained flaked tuna in spring water and
2 tablespoons coarsely chopped fresh flat-leaf parsley.
Meanwhile, cook 375g rollini pasta in large saucepan
of boiling water until tender; drain. Combine pasta with
sauce. Serve sprinkled with extra chopped parsley.
prep + cook time **35 minutes** serves **4**
nutritional count per serving **7.2g total fat**
(1.7g saturated fat); 2374kJ (568 cal);
84.6g carbohydrate; 36.5g protein; 6.6g fibre

Use any spiral-shaped pasta you like.

salmon and herb quiche

3 eggs

2 egg whites

1½ cups (375ml) skim milk

½ cup (80g) wholemeal self-raising flour

1 medium brown onion (150g), chopped finely

20g butter, melted

2 tablespoons finely chopped fresh
   flat-leaf parsley

1 tablespoon finely chopped fresh chervil

¼ cup (20g) finely grated parmesan cheese

415g can pink salmon, drained, flaked

1 Preheat oven to 180°C/160°C fan-forced. Grease deep 23cm-round fluted pie dish.

2 Whisk eggs, egg whites, milk, flour, onion, butter, herbs and cheese in large bowl until combined. Add salmon; mix gently. Pour mixture into dish.

3 Bake about 50 minutes. Stand 10 minutes before serving. Accompany with lemon wedges, if you like.

prep + cook time **1 hour 10 minutes** serves 6
nutritional count per serving **11.4g total fat** (4.8g saturated fat); 1049kJ (251 cal); 14.1g carbohydrate; 22.3g protein; 1g fibre

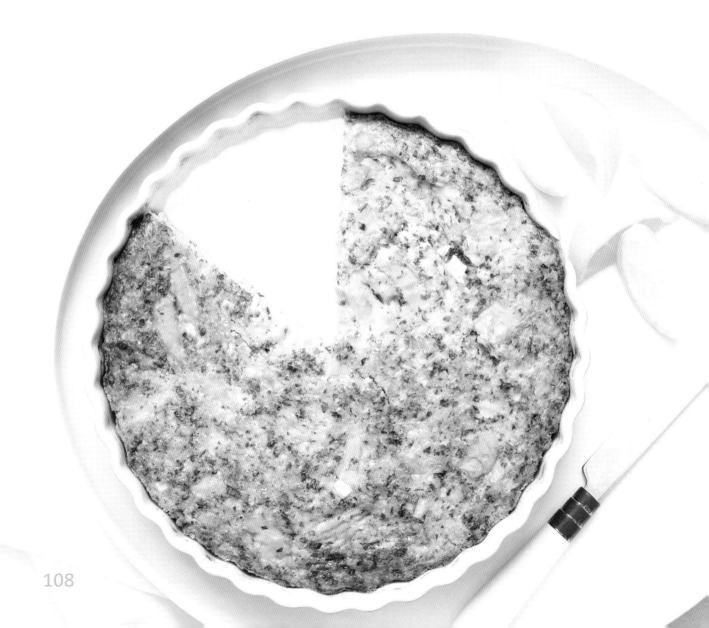

salmon, pea and risoni salad

250g risoni pasta
1 cup (120g) frozen peas
415g can red salmon, drained, flaked
100g baby spinach leaves
4 green onions, sliced thinly
dill dressing
2 tablespoons olive oil
3 teaspoons finely grated lemon rind
¼ cup (60ml) lemon juice
1 tablespoon coarsely chopped fresh dill
2 teaspoons dijon mustard
1 teaspoon caster sugar

1 Cook pasta in large saucepan of boiling water until almost tender. Add peas; cook until peas and pasta are tender; drain. Transfer to large bowl.
2 Meanwhile, make dill dressing.
3 Add salmon, spinach, onion and dressing to pasta in large bowl; mix gently.
dill dressing Combine ingredients in screw-top jar; shake well.
prep + cook time **20 minutes** serves **4**
nutritional count per serving **15.5g total fat (3g saturated fat); 1885kJ (451 cal); 46.7g carbohydrate; 28.1g protein; 4.9g fibre**

If you are unable to buy sourdough bread, making breadcrumbs from any "solid" firm-textured bread, such as turkish bread is fine; you can use sandwich, bread, if necessary, but crumb wholemeal rather than white bread.

375g orecchiette pasta
600g broccoli, cut into florets
2 teaspoons olive oil
8 drained anchovy fillets, chopped finely
2 cloves garlic, sliced thinly
2 tablespoons lemon juice
chilli crumbs
¼ cup (15g) stale sourdough breadcrumbs
1 fresh long red chilli, chopped finely

orecchiette with broccoli, anchovies and chilli crumbs

1 Cook pasta in large saucepan of boiling water until tender; drain, reserving ¼ cup cooking liquid.
2 Boil, steam or microwave broccoli until tender; drain.
3 Meanwhile, make chilli crumbs.
4 Heat oil in large frying pan; cook anchovy and garlic until anchovy begins to break up and garlic is fragrant. Add juice, pasta, broccoli and reserved cooking liquid to pan; cook, stirring, until heated through.
5 Serve pasta topped with chilli crumbs.
chilli crumbs Stir breadcrumbs in medium frying pan over medium heat until browned lightly; combine with chilli in small bowl.
prep + cook time **30 minutes** serves 4
nutritional count per serving 4.3g **total fat** (0.6g saturated fat); 1714kJ (410 cal); 97g carbohydrate; 20.1g protein; 9.7g fibre

This dish goes well with a green salad.

375g macaroni pasta
40g butter
¼ cup (35g) plain flour
2½ cups (625ml) skim milk, warmed
425g can tuna in spring water, drained, flaked
1 cup (120g) frozen peas

3 shallots (75g), chopped finely
1 tablespoon finely chopped fresh
  flat-leaf parsley
2 teaspoons finely grated lemon rind
2 tablespoons lemon juice
1 cup (120g) coarsely grated cheddar cheese
1 cup (70g) stale breadcrumbs
40g butter, chopped finely, extra

lemon tuna mornay with peas

1 Preheat oven to 180°C/160°C fan-forced.
Grease six 1½-cup (375ml) ovenproof dishes.
2 Cook pasta in large saucepan of boiling
water until tender; drain.
3 Meanwhile, melt butter in medium saucepan,
add flour; cook, stirring, until mixture bubbles
and thickens slightly. Gradually stir in milk;
cook, stirring, until sauce boils and thickens.
Combine sauce, tuna, peas, shallot, parsley,
rind, juice and pasta in large bowl.
4 Spoon mixture evenly into dishes; sprinkle
with combined cheese and breadcrumbs,
dollop with extra butter. Bake, in oven, about
30 minutes or until browned lightly. Stand
5 minutes before serving.
prep + cook time **45 minutes** serves 6
nutritional count per serving **20.6g total fat
(12.4g saturated fat); 2424kJ (580 cal);
62g carbohydrate; 33.9g protein; 4.1g fibre**

200g green beans, trimmed, halved
2 tablespoons olive oil
2 tablespoons white wine vinegar
1 tablespoon lemon juice
1 small red onion (100g), sliced thinly
4 medium egg tomatoes (600g), seeded,
  cut into thin wedges
3 hard-boiled eggs, quartered
425g can tuna in spring water,
  drained, flaked
⅓ cup (40g) seeded small black olives
⅓ cup (55g) rinsed, drained caperberries
2 tablespoons finely shredded fresh basil
1 tablespoon coarsely chopped fresh
  flat-leaf parsley

salad niçoise

1 Boil, steam or microwave beans until tender;
drain. Rinse under cold water; drain.
2 Whisk oil, vinegar and juice together in large
bowl; add beans and remaining ingredients,
mix gently.

prep + cook time 20 minutes serves 4
nutritional count per serving 16g total fat
(3.5g saturated fat); 1292kJ (309 cal);
9.6g carbohydrate; 29.6g protein; 4.2g fibre

This dish goes well with crusty bread and crackers. Serve sprinkled with extra finely chopped fresh flat-leaf parsley, if you like.

180g light cream cheese, softened
2 tablespoons lemon juice
few drops Tabasco sauce
110g can sardines in spring water, drained, mashed
1 shallot (25g), chopped finely
2 teaspoons finely chopped fresh flat-leaf parsley
¼ teaspoon cracked black pepper

sardine dip

1 Beat cream cheese, juice and sauce in small bowl with electric mixer until smooth. Stir in remaining ingredients until combined.
prep time 10 minutes serves 6 (makes 1 cup)
nutritional count per tablespoon 11.7g total fat (6.6g saturated fat); 652kJ (156 cal); 2.4g carbohydrate; 10.3g protein; 0.2g fibre

Tabasco is the brand name of an extremely fiery sauce made from vinegar and red thai chillies. Use only as much as your heat tolerance can handle.

glossary

ARAME SEAWEED available as thin, black thread-like strands from health-food stores and some supermarkets. Dry and brittle, it becomes tender once soaked – it requires a quick, light rinse then soaking for no more than 5 minutes. Avoid over-soaking as it will taste bland.

ASIAN GREENS, MIXED BABY a packaged mix of baby buk choy, choy sum, gai lan and water spinach. It is available from major supermarkets.

BACON RASHERS, SHORTCUT a "half rasher"; the streaky, narrow portion (belly) of the rasher has been removed leaving the choice eye meat.

BALMAIN BUG a shovel-shaped mollusc with flesh similar to that of a lobster. Also known as slipper or shovelnose lobster or southern bay lobster. Substitute with moreton bay bugs, king prawns or scampi.

BANANA LEAVES order from fruit and vegetable stores. Cut with a sharp knife close to the main stem, then immerse in hot water so leaves will be pliable. Foil can be used if banana leaves are unavailable.

BASIL an aromatic herb; there are many types, but the most commonly used is sweet, or common, basil.
thai also known as horapa; has small leaves, purplish stems and a slight licorice/aniseed taste. Available in Asian supermarkets and greengrocers.

BEANS
butter also known as lima beans; large, flat, kidney-shaped beans, off-white in colour, with a mealy texture and mild taste. Available canned and dried.
cannellini small white bean similar in appearance and flavour to other white beans – great northern, navy or haricot, all of which can be substituted for each other. Available dried or canned.
sprouts also known as bean shoots; tender new growths of assorted beans and seeds germinated for consumption as sprouts. The most readily available are mung bean, soya beans, alfalfa and snow pea sprouts.

BREADCRUMBS
japanese also known as panko, these breadcrumbs have a lighter texture than western-style breadcrumbs, and give a crunchy texture with a delicate, pale golden colour. Available from Asian grocery stores. Substitute with coarse breadcrumbs made from quite stale or gently toasted white bread.
sourdough made by blending or processing day-old sourdough bread.
stale one- or two-day-old bread made into crumbs by blending or processing.

BUTTER use salted or unsalted (sweet) butter; 125g is equal to one stick (4 ounces) of butter.

BUTTERMILK originally the term given to slightly sour liquid left after butter was churned from cream, today it is made similarly to yogurt. Sold alongside all fresh milk products in supermarkets. Despite the implication of its name, it is low in fat.

CALAMARI a type of squid.

CAPERBERRIES fruit formed after the caper buds have flowered; caperberries are pickled, usually with stalks intact. Available from some delicatessens.

CAPERS the grey-green buds of a warm climate (usually Mediterranean) shrub, sold either dried and salted or pickled in a vinegar brine. Baby capers, those picked early, are fuller-flavoured and more expensive than the full-sized ones. Rinse well before using.

CAPSICUM also known as bell pepper or, simply, pepper. Can be red, green, yellow, orange or purplish black. Seeds and membranes should be discarded before use. Also available, roasted, bottled in oil or brine.

CAYENNE PEPPER a long, thin-fleshed, extremely hot red chilli usually sold dried and ground.

CHEESE
cream cheese commonly known as Philadelphia or Philly, a soft cows-milk cheese with a fat content of at least 33%. Also available as light cream cheese; a blend of cottage and cream cheeses with a fat content of 21%.
gouda mild cream-coloured Dutch cheese made from cows milk. Has a mild nutty flavour. Shaped in rounds.

CHERVIL also known as cicely; a herb with a mild fennel flavour.

CIABATTA in Italian, the word means "slipper", which is the traditional shape of this popular crisp-crusted white bread.

CHICKPEAS also called garbanzos, channa or hummus; a round, sandy-coloured legume.

CHILLI available in many different types and sizes. Use rubber gloves when seeding and chopping fresh chillies as they can burn your skin. Removing seeds and membranes lessens the heat level.
flakes, dried deep-red, dehydrated chilli slices and whole seeds.
green any unripened chilli; also some varieties that are green when ripe.
long red available fresh and dried; a generic term used for any moderately hot, long (6-8cm), thin chilli.
thai also known as "scuds"; small, hot and bright red in colour.

COLD-SMOKED FISH see hot-smoked.

CORIANDER when fresh is also known as pak chee, cilantro or chinese parsley; a bright-green-leafed herb with a pungent flavour. Both stems and roots of coriander are also used in cooking. Wash well under cold water to remove any dirt clinging to the roots, then scrape the roots with a small flat knife to remove some of the outer fibrous skin. Chop coriander roots and stems together to obtain the amount specified. Also available ground or as seeds; these should not be substituted for fresh coriander as the tastes are completely different.

CORNFLOUR also known as cornstarch; used as a thickening agent in cooking.

CORNICHONS French for gherkin; a very small variety of cucumber.

CUCUMBER
lebanese short, slender and thin-skinned. Probably the most popular variety because of its tender, edible skin, tiny, yielding seeds and sweet, fresh and flavoursome taste.
telegraph also known as the european or burpless cucumber; slender and long (35cm and more), its thin dark-green skin has shallow ridges running down its length.

CUMIN also known as zeera or comino; has a spicy, nutty flavour. Available in seed form or dried and ground.

CURRANTS, DRIED tiny, almost black raisins, so-named after a grape variety that originated in Corinth, Greece.

CURRY
leaves available fresh or dried from greengrocers and Asian grocery stores. Has a mild curry flavour; use like bay leaves.
powder a blend of ground spices that may include dried chilli, cinnamon, cumin, coriander, fennel, fenugreek, mace, cardamom and turmeric. Can be mild or hot.

CURRY PASTES some recipes in this book call for commercially prepared pastes of various strength and flavours. Use whichever one you feel suits your spice-level tolerance best.
red curry paste a hot blend of flavours that include thai chilli, garlic, shallot, lemon grass, galangal, shrimp paste, kaffir lime peel, coriander, cumin and paprika. It is milder than the hotter thai green curry paste.

CUTTLEFISH is a type of mollusc known as a cephalopod, which also includes squid and octopus.

DAIKON a giant radish with a sweet, fresh flavour. The flesh is crisp, juicy and white, while the skin can be either creamy white or black. It can range from 15cm to 38cm in length, with an average diameter of 5-7.5cm. Should be firm and unwrinkled. Refrigerate, wrapped in a plastic bag, for up to a week.

DASHI a basic fish and seaweed stock. Made from dried bonito (tuna) flakes and kombu (kelp). Instant dashi powder, also known as dashi-no-moto, is a concentrated granulated powder. Available from Asian grocery stores.

EGGPLANTS, BABY also known as finger or japanese eggplant.

FENNEL also known as finocchio or anise; a white to very pale green-white, firm, crisp, roundish vegetable about 8-12cm in diameter. The bulb has a slightly sweet, anise flavour but the leaves have a much stronger taste. Also the name given to dried seeds having a licorice flavour.

FIRM WHITE FISH FILLETS blue-eye, bream, flathead, ling, whiting, jewfish, swordfish, snapper or sea perch are all good choices. Remove any small bones in the fillets with tweezers.

FIVE-SPICE POWDER a fragrant mix of ground cinnamon, cloves, star anise, sichuan pepper and fennel seeds. Also known as chinese five-spice.

FLOUR
plain an all-purpose flour made from wheat.
self-raising plain flour sifted with baking powder in the proportion of 1 cup plain flour to 2 teaspoons baking powder.
wholemeal also known as wholewheat flour; flour milled from whole wheat grain (bran, germ and flour).

GARAM MASALA a blend of roasted spices based on varying proportions of cloves, cardamom, cinnamon, cumin, coriander and fennel.

GINGER also known as green or root ginger; thick root of a tropical plant.

HOT-SMOKED FISH is smoked for a short time at an extremely high temperature, which is hot enough to cook it. In cold-smoking, smoke is circulated over the fish at a low temperature for a relatively long period of time. The finished product is uncooked, leaving the texture unchanged. When a recipe askes for "smoked fish", it is the thinly sliced, cold-smoked fish that is used.

KAFFIR LIME LEAF also known as bai magrood; looks like two glossy dark green leaves joined end to end, forming a rounded hourglass shape. A strip of fresh lime peel may be substituted for each kaffir lime leaf.

KECAP MANIS see sauces.

KITCHEN STRING made of a natural product, such as cotton or hemp, so that it neither affects the flavour of the food it's tied around, nor melts when heated.

KUMARA Polynesian name of orange-fleshed sweet potato often confused with yam.

LEMON GRASS a tall, clumping, lemon-smelling and -tasting, sharp-edged grass; the white lower part of the stem is chopped before using.

LEMON MYRTLE an aromatic plant native to Australia having a lemon-grass-like flavour. Available from specialist food stores.

LEMON THYME a herb with a lemony scent, which is due to the high level of citral in its leaves. The citrus scent is enhanced by crushing the leaves in your hands before using the herb.

LENTILS, AUSTRALIAN GREEN tiny, green-blue lentils with a nutty, earthy flavour. A fast-cooking pulse that holds up well through boiling – it doesn't disintegrate like other lentils. Originally grown in France (lentils du puy), they are now grown in Australia and may also be sold as french green lentils, bondi lentils or matilda lentils.

MESCLUN a salad mix of assorted young lettuce and other green leaves, including baby spinach, mizuna and curly endive.

MIRIN a Japanese champagne-coloured cooking wine that is used expressly for cooking and should not be confused with sake.

MISO Japan's famous thick bean paste made from fermented soya beans and grains. It varies in colour, texture and saltiness. White miso is a pale yellow paste; it is the sweetest and mildest of them all. Available from Asian food stores.

MUSHROOMS
shiitake when fresh is also known as chinese black or forest mushrooms; although cultivated, they have the earthy taste of wild mushrooms. When dried they are known as donko or dried chinese mushrooms; rehydrate before use.
swiss brown also known as cremini or roman; light to dark brown mushrooms with a full-bodied flavour. Button or cup mushrooms can be substituted.

MUSSELS a bivalve mollusc; must be tightly closed when bought, indicating they are alive. Before cooking, scrub the shells with a strong brush and remove the "beards". Discard any shells that do not open during cooking.

NOODLES
bean thread also known as wun sen, cellophane or glass noodles because they are transparent when cooked. Must be soaked to soften before use.

hokkien also known as stir-fry noodles; fresh wheat noodles that resemble thick, yellow-brown spaghetti. It needs no pre-cooking before being used.

rice stick comes in different widths – thin used in soups, wide in stir-fries – but all should be soaked in hot water until soft.

soba thin spaghetti-like pale brown noodle from Japan made from buckwheat and wheat flours.

somen very thin, white, Japanese noodles made of wheat flour; are the thinnest of all Japanese noodles. In Japan, somen is most often served cold, usually with a dipping sauce (rather than as part of a hot soup).

udon available fresh and dried; these broad, white, Japanese wheat noodles are similar to the ones in homemade chicken noodle soup.

OLIVES, SICILIAN are smooth and fine-skinned, crisp and crunchy, and have a piquant, buttery flavour. Available from good delicatessens.

ONION

green also known as scallion or, incorrectly, shallot; an immature onion picked before the bulb has formed, having a long, bright-green edible stalk.

red also known as spanish, red spanish or bermuda onion; a sweet-flavoured, large, purple-red onion.

shallots also called french shallots, golden shallots or eschalots; small, brown-skinned, elongated members of the onion family.

spring onions with small white bulbs, and long, narrow green-leafed tops.

OYSTERS a bivalve mollusc available in many varieties, including pacific, bay, blacklip and sydney or new zealand rock oyster.

PAPAYAS, GREEN are just unripe papayas. They are available at Asian food stores; look for one that is hard and slightly shiny, proving it is freshly picked. Papaya will ripen rapidly if not used within a day or two.

PAPRIKA a ground, dried, sweet red capsicum (bell pepper); there are many types available including sweet, hot, mild and smoked.

PARSLEY, FLAT-LEAF also known as continental or italian parsley.

PIPIS small smooth-shelled triangular shaped bivalve mollusc.

POLENTA also known as cornmeal; a flour-like cereal made of dried corn (maize); also the name of the dish made from it.

POTATOES, KIPFLER small, finger-shaped potato with a nutty flavour.

PRAWNS also known as shrimp.

PRESERVED LEMON RIND a North African specialty; lemons are quartered and preserved in salt and lemon juice or water. To use, remove and discard pulp, squeeze juice from rind, rinse rind well then slice thinly. Once opened, store under refrigeration.

QUINOA pronounced keen-wa. The seed of a leafy plant similar to spinach. Is gluten-free and thought to be safe for people with coeliac disease. Its cooking qualities are similar to rice, having a slightly nutty taste and chewy texture. Available from most health-food stores. Keep, sealed in a glass jar, under refrigeration, as it spoils easily.

ROCKET also known as arugula, rugula and rucola. Baby rocket leaves, also known as wild rocket, are less peppery.

SAKE Japan's favourite alcoholic drink; a rice wine that's also used in cooking. If unavailable, dry sherry, vermouth or brandy can be used as substitutes.

SAMBAL OELEK Indonesian in origin; a salty paste made from ground chillies and vinegar.

SASHIMI use the freshest, sashimi-quality fish you can find. Raw fish sold as sashimi has to meet stringent guidelines regarding its handling and treatment after leaving the water. We suggest you seek advice from local authorities before eating raw seafood.

SAUCES

fish also called nam pla or nuoc nam; made from pulverised fermented fish, most often anchovies. Has a pungent smell and strong taste; use sparingly.

hoisin a thick, sweet and spicy chinese sauce made from salted fermented soya beans, onions and garlic.

oyster Asian in origin, this rich, brown sauce is made from oysters and their brine, cooked with salt and soy sauce, and thickened with starches.

soy made from fermented soya beans. Several variations are available in most supermarkets.

dark soy is deep brown, almost black in colour; rich, with a thicker consistency than other types. Pungent but not particularly salty.

kecap manis a dark, thick, sweet soy sauce. Depending on the brand, the soy's sweetness is derived from the addition of either molasses or palm sugar when brewed.

light soy fairly thin in consistency and, while paler than the others, is the saltiest tasting. Don't confuse with salt-reduced or low-sodium soy sauces.

Tabasco brand name of an extremely fiery sauce made from vinegar and red thai chillies.

SCALLOPS a bivalve mollusc with a fluted shell valve; may or may not have the coral (roe) attached.

SILVER BEET also known as swiss chard, blettes and, mistakenly, spinach.

SPINACH also known as english spinach and, incorrectly, silver beet.

SQUID also known as calamari; a type of mollusc. Buy squid hoods to make preparation and cooking faster.

SUGAR

caster also known as superfine or finely granulated table sugar.

palm sugar also known as nam tan pip, jaggery, jawa or gula melaka; made from the sap of the sugar palm tree. Light brown to black in colour and usually sold in rock-hard cakes. If palm sugar is unavailable use brown sugar instead.

VIETNAMESE MINT not a mint at all, but a pungent and peppery narrow-leafed member of the buckwheat family; also known as cambodian mint and laksa leaf. It is available from Asian greengrocers.

WOMBOK also known as peking cabbage, chinese cabbage or petsai. Elongated in shape with pale green, crinkly leaves, this is the most common cabbage in South-East Asia.

ZUCCHINI also known as courgette; small green, yellow or white vegetable belonging to the squash family. When harvested young, its flowers are edible and can be stuffed and deep-fried.

conversion chart

MEASURES

One Australian metric measuring cup holds approximately 250ml; one Australian metric tablespoon holds 20ml; one Australian metric teaspoon holds 5ml.

The difference between one country's measuring cups and another's is within a two- or three-teaspoon variance, and will not affect your cooking results. North America, New Zealand and the United Kingdom use a 15ml tablespoon.

All cup and spoon measurements are level. The most accurate way of measuring dry ingredients is to weigh them. When measuring liquids, use a clear glass or plastic jug with the metric markings.

We use large eggs with an average weight of 60g.

DRY MEASURES

METRIC	IMPERIAL
15g	½oz
30g	1oz
60g	2oz
90g	3oz
125g	4oz (¼lb)
155g	5oz
185g	6oz
220g	7oz
250g	8oz (½lb)
280g	9oz
315g	10oz
345g	11oz
375g	12oz (¾lb)
410g	13oz
440g	14oz
470g	15oz
500g	16oz (1lb)
750g	24oz (1½lb)
1kg	32oz (2lb)

LIQUID MEASURES

METRIC	IMPERIAL
30ml	1 fluid oz
60ml	2 fluid oz
100ml	3 fluid oz
125ml	4 fluid oz
150ml	5 fluid oz (¼ pint/1 gill)
190ml	6 fluid oz
250ml	8 fluid oz
300ml	10 fluid oz (½ pint)
500ml	16 fluid oz
600ml	20 fluid oz (1 pint)
1000ml (1 litre)	1¾ pints

LENGTH MEASURES

METRIC	IMPERIAL
3mm	⅛ in
6mm	¼in
1cm	½in
2cm	¾in
2.5cm	1in
5cm	2in
6cm	2½in
8cm	3in
10cm	4in
13cm	5in
15cm	6in
18cm	7in
20cm	8in
23cm	9in
25cm	10in
28cm	11in
30cm	12in (1ft)

OVEN TEMPERATURES

These oven temperatures are only a guide for conventional ovens. For fan-forced ovens, check the manufacturer's manual.

	°C (CELSIUS)	°F (FAHRENHEIT)	GAS MARK
Very slow	120	250	½
Slow	150	275-300	1-2
Moderately slow	160	325	3
Moderate	180	350-375	4-5
Moderately hot	200	400	6
Hot	220	425-450	7-8
Very hot	240	475	9

index

ACP BOOKS

General manager Christine Whiston
Editor-in-chief Susan Tomnay
Creative director & designer Hieu Chi Nguyen
Art director Hannah Blackmore
Senior editor Wendy Bryant
Food writer Xanthe Roberts
Food director Pamela Clark
Test Kitchen manager + nutritional information Belinda Farlow
Recipe development Nicole Jennings, Kate Nichols
Sales & rights director Brian Cearnes
Marketing manager Bridget Cody
Senior business analyst Rebecca Varela
Circulation manager Jama Mclean
Operations manager David Scotto
Production manager Victoria Jefferys

ACP Books are published by ACP Magazines a division of
PBL Media Pty Limited

PBL Media, Chief Executive Officer Ian Law
Publishing & sales director, Women's lifestyle Lynette Phillips
Group editorial director, Women's lifestyle Pat Ingram
Marketing director, Women's lifestyle Matthew Dominello
Commercial manager, Women's lifestyle Seymour Cohen
Research director, Women's lifestyle Justin Stone

Produced by ACP Books, Sydney.

Published by ACP Books, a division of ACP Magazines Ltd, 54 Park St, Sydney; GPO Box 4088, Sydney, NSW 2001.
phone (02) 9282 8618; fax (02) 9267 9438; acpbooks@acpmagazines.com.au; www.acpbooks.com.au

Printed by Toppan Printing Co., China.

Australia Distributed by Network Services, phone +61 2 9282 8777; fax +61 2 9264 3278;
networkweb@networkservicescompany.com.au
United Kingdom Distributed by Australian Consolidated Press (UK), phone (01604) 642 200;
fax (01604) 642 300; books@acpuk.com
New Zealand Distributed by Netlink Distribution Company, phone (9) 366 9966; ask@ndc.co.nz
South Africa Distributed by PSD Promotions, phone (27 11) 392 6065/6/7;
fax (27 11) 392 6079/80; orders@psdprom.co.za
Canada Distributed by Publishers Group Canada
phone (800) 663 5714; fax (800) 565 3770; service@raincoast.com

Title: Hooked on fish / food director Pamela Clark.
ISBN: 978 1 86396 861 4 (pbk.)
Notes: Includes index.
Subjects: Cookery (Seafood).
Other Authors/Contributors: Clark, Pamela.
Dewey Number: 641.692

Scanpan cookware is used in the AWW Test Kitchen.
The publishers would like to thank the following for props used in photography:
Alfresco Emporium, Bed Bath N' Table, Clay & Flax, Country Road, Domayne Alexandria,
hart & heim, IKEA Jarass Pty Ltd, Jedo's Beach House, Major & Tom, Maxwell & Williams,
No Chintz, Prop Stop, Rapee, Sheldon & Hammond, Stoneage Ceramics,
The Bay Tree, The Essential Ingredient, Tomkin Australia.

Send recipe enquiries to: recipeenquiries@acpmagazines.com.au